Mac Bride

TEACH YOURSELF BOOKS

Orders: please contact Bookpoint Ltd, 39 Milton Park, Abingdon, Oxon OX14 4TD. Telephone: (44) 01235 400414, Fax: (44) 01235 400454. Lines are open 9.00–6.00, Monday to Saturday, with a 24-hour message answering service. E-mail address: orders@bookpoint.co.uk

Long renowned as the authoritative source for self-guided learning – with more than 30 million copies sold worldwide – the *Teach Yourself* series includes over 200 titles in the fields of languages, crafts, hobbies, business and education.

British Library Cataloguing in Publication Data
A catalogue record for this title is available from The British Library

ISBN 0 340 738 235

First published 1988
Impression number   10   9   8   7   6   5   4   3   2
Year   2004   2003   2002   2001   2000   1999

The 'Teach Yourself' name and logo are registered trade marks of Hodder & Stoughton Ltd.

Cover photo from the Daily Telegraph Colour Library

Typeset by MacDesign, Southampton
Printed in Great Britain for Hodder & Stoughton Educational, a division of Hodder Headline Plc, 338 Euston Road, London NW1 3BH by Cox & Wyman Ltd, Reading, Berkshire.

CONTENTS

PREFACE

Windows 98 is the latest version of Microsoft's world-beating operating system, and one that takes another step further along the path of making computers easier to use.

Teach Yourself Windows 98 is written primarily for those people who are new to computers, or are at least new to the Windows way – if you have previously used Windows 95, the change to 98 is very simple. This book introduces the basic concepts of working with **W**indows (the system) and **w**indows (the framed parts of the screen in which programs run). It will show you how to set up your computer to suit the way you like to work – you can control more or less everything from the screen display down to the speed of the mouse's response! You will find out how to manage your files efficiently, organising your storage so that you can find things quickly and removing unwanted clutter, and how to care for your disks so they continue to perform well for a long time.

The Windows package includes many accessories and applications, both large and small. We will be looking briefly at some of these, and more closely at Internet Explorer and Outlook Express. With these two tools you can browse and download files from the Internet, and handle e-mail and newsgroup articles. Windows 98 has been designed for easy Internet access, in fact, integration with the Internet is central to its design. If you choose, and if you have the hardware and the connections to support it, you can almost treat the Internet as an extension of your desktop.

This book does not aim to cover every single aspect of Windows 98, for two very good reasons. There is far too much to fit into 200 or so pages, and few people will ever use all its features. *Teach Yourself Windows 98* concentrates on the needs of the new user at home and in the office. It aims to cover the things that you need to know to be able to use your computer efficiently, and things that you might like to know because they can make using your computer more enjoyable. Working with Windows is intuitive – once you know how to 'intuit'! When you have mastered the basics and become familiar with some applications, you should be able to apply your understanding of the 'Windows way' to any other Windows applications that interest you.

Happy Windowing

Mac Bride

1998

1 | INTRODUCING WINDOWS 98

1.1 Aims of this chapter

Windows 98 is very easy to use – once you have mastered a few key skills and concepts. This chapter gives an overview of Windows 98 and of how it works. It looks at what you see on screen, and how you can respond to it and control it with the mouse and keyboard. It also introduces some essential terminology and the ideas behind them.

If you have previously used any similar computer system – such as Windows 95, NT or 3.1, or Apple Macintosh – you can skim through the next few pages, or skip them altogether, and go straight to Chapter 2.

1.2 What is Windows 98?

Windows 98 is an *operating system* – and more. An operating system handles the low-level interaction between the processor and the screen, memory, mouse, disk drives, printer and other peripherals. Windows 98 has *drivers* (control programs) for all PC-compatible processors and just about every kind of PC peripheral currently on the market – and for some that are still being developed! The operating system is a bridge between the hardware of the computer and the *applications* – such as word-processor, spreadsheet or Internet browser. As a result, whatever hardware you are using, as long as it can run the Windows 98 operating system, it can run any Windows 98 application. (It will also be able to run applications written for earlier versions of Windows.)

Although the operating system is the most important part of Windows, most of it is invisible to you. You don't even need to think about how it works or what it does as Windows 98 has its own routines for checking and maintaining the operating system.

Plug and Play

These built-in maintenance routines also come into play when you add new hardware, such as a joystick, scanner or extra hard drive, to your PC. Windows 98 will normally recognise their presence automatically, and install the software needed to control them. This 'plug and play' approach, introduced with Windows 95, is a vast improvement on earlier operating systems – with those, you could spend hours trying to get the computer to work with new hardware!

The Desktop

The most visible part of Windows 98 is, of course, the screen or *Desktop*, as it is called. Windows is a graphical system. It uses *icons* (small images) to represent programs and files, and visual displays to show what is happening inside your computer. Many of the routine jobs are done by clicking on, dragging (see page 7) or otherwise manipulating these images, using the mouse or keyboard.

Windows is *multi-tasking* – it can run any number of programs at once. In practice, only a few will normally be active at the same time but that is more a reflection of the human inability to do several jobs simultaneously! A typical example of multi-tasking would be one program downloading material from the Internet and another printing a long report, while you wrote a letter in a third.

Each program runs in a separate area of the screen – a window – and these can be resized, moved, minimised or overlapped however you like. Managing windows is covered in Chapter 3.

Utilities and accessories

Apart from the operating system, Windows 98 contains a large set of programs. Some of these are utilities for managing the system – organising file storage on the disk, adding new peripherals or fine-tuning the way that they work. Others are applications for your use and amusement. There's *WordPad*, a good word-processor, *Paint* and *Imaging*, for creating graphics, a *Calculator*, *Phone Dialer*, some games, a set of multimedia tools and applications for the Internet, including Internet Explorer. All of the essential utilities and the more useful applications are covered in this book.

Integration with the Internet

Windows 98 offers a very high level of integration with the Internet – it can become almost an extension of your Desktop. This integration works best within organisations that are connected to the Internet through an ISDN line, giving fast, easy access – and preferably with the line open all the time.

If you connect through a dial-up line – as most home and small business users do – you cannot move smoothly from the Desktop to the Internet. In this situation, you will probably 'go online' (connect to the Internet) once or twice a day to get your e-mail or browse the Web, and this will be quite separate from your other computing activities. If you do not have Internet access, these aspects of Windows 98 are superfluous.

1.3 The Desktop

The screen should be treated as if it really were a desktop. This is where you keep your tools – utilities and applications – and you can arrange things so that those tools you use most often are close at hand. This is where you create your documents – and you may have several under way at the same time, in the same or in separate applications. You can arrange these so that you can read two or more at once if you want to compare them or copy material from one to another. If you have finished with an application for the time being, you can tuck it out of the way – but still ready to be restarted with a click.

What's on the Desktop?

What do you see when you look at the screen? The answer will vary, of course, depending upon what you are doing and how you have set up the system, but some or all of these items should be visible.

Background

This may be a flat colour, a pattern, a picture or a Web page with text and images. It can be changed at any time without affecting anything else.

Shortcuts

These are icons with links to programs, to *folders* (for storing files on the hard disk) or to places on the Internet. Clicking on the icon will run the

Shortcuts   Application windows   Background

Start menu   Document   Clock

Quick Launch toolbar   Application buttons   Taskbar

Figure 1.1 The **Desktop**, in Classic mode (see Chapter 2), showing some of the main features.

program, open the folder or take you off into the Internet. There are some shortcuts there already, but you can easily add your own (see page 81).

Taskbar

This is normally present as a strip along the bottom of the screen, though it can be moved elsewhere (Chapter 9). It is the main control centre for the Desktop, carrying the tools and buttons to start and to switch between applications.

Start menu

Clicking on the **Start** button, on the left of the Taskbar, opens the Start menu. Any application on your system can be run from here. The menu also leads to recently-used documents, favourite places on the Internet, the Help pages and other utilities.

Quick Launch toolbar

Shortcuts can be obscured by application windows, but the Taskbar is normally always visible. The Quick Launch toolbar is just one of the toolbars that can be added to the Taskbar to give you ready access to applications, no matter what the state of the Desktop.

Internet Explorer   View Channels

Outlook Express   Show Desktop

Three of the tools here lead to your main Internet applications (see Chapter 10). The fourth, Show Desktop, shrinks all open applications out of the way so that you have a clear view of the Desktop.

Clock

This is optional, but useful. You should find that the clock keeps excellent time – it even adjusts itself at the start and end of Summer Time!

THE TASKBAR

The Start menu, Quick Launch toolbar and Clock are all dealt with in more detail along with the other Taskbar features, in Chapter 9.

Application windows

When you run an application, such as Windows Explorer (Chapter 7), WordPad, Paint or the Calculator (all in Chapter 14), it is displayed in a window. This can be set to fill the screen or to take a smaller area so that part of the Desktop is visible beneath (see Chapter 3 for more on windows).

Application buttons

When you run an application, a button is added to the Taskbar. Clicking on it will bring that application to the top of your Desktop.

Document

The letter that you are writing in WordPad, the picture in Paint, the budget you have set out in a spreadsheet – all of these are *documents*. A document is normally only seen in the application that created it, or a compatible one. In the screenshot on page 4, the document 'desktop.doc' is open in Microsoft Word.

CUSTOMISING THE DESKTOP

The appearance of the Desktop and the way that you interact with it can be changed to suit yourself. See Chapter 2 to find out how to do this.

1.4 The mouse

The mouse is almost essential for work with Windows – you can manage without it, but not as easily. It is used for selecting and manipulating objects, highlighting text, making choices, and clicking icons and buttons – as well as for playing games and for drawing in graphics applications.

There are five 'moves' that you should master.

Point

The easy one! Move the mouse so that the tip of the arrow cursor (or the finger of the hand cursor) is over the object you want to point to. If you point to an icon, and hold the cursor there for a moment, a label will appear, telling you what the icon stands for.

Click

A single click of the left mouse button.

Double-click

Two clicks, in quick succession, of the left mouse button. The response of the mouse can be adjusted to suit your double-click speed (see page 103).

Right-click

A single click of the right mouse button.

Drag

Point to an object or place on the Desktop, hold down the left mouse button and draw the cursor across the screen.

1.5 The keyboard

The keyboard is mainly for entering text, but can also be used for editing text and controlling the system. These keys, in particular, are worth identifying and remembering:

Windows – press to open the Start menu. Also used in some keyboard shortcuts.

Control – used in combination with other keys for shortcuts to menu commands.

Alt – mainly used for menu selections (page 9).

Application – displays the shortcut menu of a selected item (page 9).

The **Enter** keys, used after entering text or to make selections.

The first of the **Function** keys. This one always calls up Help. The others do different jobs, depending upon the application.

Backspace – deletes the selected object on screen or the letter to the left in a block of text.

Delete – deletes the selected object on screen or the letter to the right in a block of text.

Jump to the top/bottom of a block of text or a window display.

Scroll up/down one window length.

Move through text, menus and folder displays. Can sometimes be combined with Control for faster movement.

1.6 Menus

In any Windows 98 (or earlier) applications, the commands and options are grouped on a set of pull-down menus.

They follow simple rules:

- If an item has an ▶ on the right, a submenu will open when you point to the item.
- If an item has ... after the name, a panel or dialog box (page 12) will open when you point to the item.
- If an item has ● to its left, it is the selected option from a set.
- If an item has ✓ to its left, it is an option and is turned on – click to turn it off or on again.
- If a name is written in grey ('greyed out'), the command is not available at that time – you probably have to select something first.

Menus and the mouse

- To open a menu, click on its name in the Menu bar.
- To run a command or set an option click on it with the mouse.
- To leave the menu system without selecting a command, click anywhere else on the screen.

Figure 1.2 A typical menu (this is in Windows Explorer).

Menu selection using the keyboard

When the work that you are doing is mainly typing, you may find it more convenient to make your menu selections via the keyboard. Here's how:

1 Hold down **Alt** and press the underlined letter in the name on the Menu bar.

Either

2 Press the underlined letter of the name to run the command, set the on/off option or open the sub-menu.

Or

2 Move through the menus with the arrow keys – up/down the menu and right to open sub-menus – then press **Enter**.

■ The left/right arrows will move you from one menu to another.

■ Press **Escape** to close the menu without selecting a command.

Keyboard shortcuts

Many applications allow you to activate some of the most commonly-used commands directly from the keyboard, without touching the menu system. For example, in Paint **Control** + **S** (i.e. hold down a **Control** key and press **S**) will call up the **Save** command; **Control** + **O** has the same effect as selecting **Open** from the **File** menu.

The shortcuts vary, and some applications will offer far more than others, but some are common to all – or most – applications. If a command has a keyboard shortcut, it will be shown on the menu, to the right of the name.

1.7 Shortcut menus

If you right-click on more or less anything on the screen, or press the **Application** key when an object is selected, a menu will appear beside or on the object. This is its *shortcut* or *context menu* – it will contain a set of commands and options that are relevant to the object in that context. Right-click on a shortcut to a folder, on a shortcut to an application, on the Taskbar

Figure 1.3 Three examples of shortcut menus, from **(A)** Online services, **(B)** My Documents and **(C)** the Desktop.

or on the background and see what comes up. Don't worry at this stage about what the commands and options do, just notice how they vary – and that some are present on many menus.

1.8 Properties, dialog boxes and options

Almost every object in the Windows 98 system has *Properties*, which define what it looks like and how it works. These can be seen, and often changed, through the Properties panel. This is normally reached through the context menu – notice how all the menus is Figure 1.3 have Properties as the last item.

Properties panels often have several *tabs*, each dealing with a different aspect of the object. The contents vary enormously. Some will simply contain information – such as the size, date and other details of a file – others have options that you can set in different ways.

■ To switch between tabs, click on the name at the top.

When a Windows program wants to get information from you, it will do it through a *dialog box*. These vary in size and style, depending upon the information to be collected.

Windows uses a range of methods for setting options and collecting information in its Properties panels and dialog boxes.

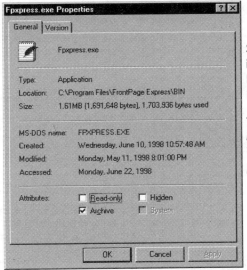

Some tabs are purely for information. This one also has some options in the bottom section.

Tip: As a general rule, leave the Attributes alone! The default settings are probably best.

Click on the name to open a tab.

Options can be set in many ways (see page 10).

When you have finished with a panel, click **OK** to fix your changes, or **Cancel** to leave things as they were before. **Apply** will make the changes but leave the panel open.

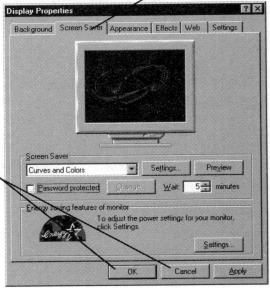

Figure 1.4 Two **Properties** panels. The top one is from a program, the bottom one from the Desktop (see Chapter 2).

Drop down list
(open) – select
from the list

Text box – enter
the information

Drop down list (closed).

Figure 1.5 A **Save As** dialog box showing an open drop-down list and a text box. The **Save as type** options are also on a drop-down list.

Text boxes

Typically used for collecting filenames or personal details. Sometimes a value will be suggested by the system. Edit it, or retype it if necessary.

Drop-down lists

These look like text boxes but have an arrow to their right. Click on the arrow to make the list drop down, then select a value.

Lists

With a simple list, just scroll through it and select a value. They sometimes have a linked text box. The selected value is displayed there, but you can also type in a value.

Check boxes

These are switches for options – click to turn them on or off. Check boxes are sometimes found singly, but often

in sets. You can have any number of check box options turned on at the same time, unlike radio buttons.

Radio buttons

These are used to select one – and only one – from a set of alternatives. Click on the button or its name to select.

Sliders and number values

Sliders are used where an approximate value will do – for example, volume controls, speed and colour definition (actual values may not mean much to the average user in these situations!). Clicking

to the side of the slider will move it towards the click point, or you can drag the slider in the direction.

Numbers are often set through little scroll boxes. Click the up/down arrows to change the value. If you want to change the value significantly it is often quicker to type it in.

1.9 Summary

- Windows 98 is an operating system with an accompanying package of utility and application programs.
- The screen is referred to as the Desktop, and should be treated much as a real desktop.
- The mouse responds to single and double clicks of the left button, and to single clicks of the right button. It can also be used to drag objects across the Desktop.
- Certain keys serve specific functions.
- In any application, the commands can be reached through the menu system.
- Regularly-used commands often have keyboard shortcuts.
- Right-clicking on an object normally opens a shortcut menu, containing relevant commands.
- Windows 98 has a number of simple ways to set options and make selections.

2 | THE DESKTOP

2.1 Aims of this chapter

In this chapter we will look at the Desktop itself, and ways to arrange items on it – experimenting will show you what works best for you in different situations. We will also look at how you can change the appearance of the Desktop, as you should set the screen up to suit yourself before you go any further into your explorations of Windows 98.

2.2 Desktop modes

The Desktop can be run in two modes – or a combination of the two – which affect both the appearance and the way that you handle items. You can switch between the modes at any time.

Web Page mode

In this mode, the shortcuts are underlined and respond to a single click. This is the *Active Desktop*, from which you can reach out into the Internet through channels and other interactive components.

Channels

A normal Internet link will connect you to a site so that you can pull information down from it. Channels also link to Web sites, but on a *push* basis. If you subscribe to a channel, it will send pages to you whenever they are updated. This can be done automatically, at scheduled times, and you can browse elsewhere on the Internet – or do something else – while the files come in. The pages can then be read later, when you are offline.

The Channel Bar offers a simple way to subscribe to a dozen popular channels – these are not active until you subscribe – and you can choose from thousands more online at Microsoft's Channel Guide.

Channel Bar

Notice the underlines   Active Desktop component

Figure 2.1 The **Desktop**, in Web page mode.

■ Subscription to a Channel does not usually cost anything (though a few specialist business services do charge).

Active Desktop components

These are another form of link to Web sites, and are typically interactive. A good example is the Microsoft Search component, which allows you to set up a search at any one of dozens of sites before you go online.

Classic mode

In this simpler mode, it takes a double-click to start a shortcut, and the Channel Bar and other Active Desktop components are not displayed. If you do not have an Internet connection, or you find that you do not make use of the Active Desktop features, this is the mode to use.

2.3 Customising the Desktop

The customised Desktop can be based on either the Web page or Classic mode. You can change the settings – and go back and adjust them – at any point without affecting any other application that may be open at the time.

1 Right-click anywhere on the background of the Desktop to get its context menu.

2 The top command, **Active Desktop**, leads to a submenu. Point to it to open the sub-menu and select **Customize my Desktop**.

3 This opens the **Display Properties** panel, with the **Web** tab at the front.

Figure 2.2 Customising the Desktop. This has already been given a new background. Also, the Taskbar has been moved to the top of the screen and the Desktop toolbar added to it. This duplicates the icons on the Desktop – useful, as it means can still reach them when an application covers the whole Desktop. (See Chapter 9 for more on the Taskbar.)

The main option here is **View my Active Desktop as a web page**. If that is turned on, you can then select which Active Desktop elements you want to include.

At first, there will only be one element listed – Internet Explorer Channel Bar. Over time you may add many elements, with the effect that the screen becomes impossibly crowded if they are all visible at once. Using this panel to turn them off is the equivalent of clearing stuff off your desk and piling it on the floor (though a bit more organised). The elements are still available and can be turned back on at any time.

We will look at how to add Active Desktop elements in Chapter 10.

Click to open the Folder Options panel

Figure 2.3 The Web tab. The **New** and **Delete** button refer to Active Desktop elements. If you click the **Apply** button, the new settings will be applied without closing the panel.

Near the bottom of the panel is the **Folder Options** button. Click this. You will be asked if you want to close the Desktop Properties panel and open the Folder Options panel – you do, so click **Yes**.

Folder Options

At this point we are only interested in the **General** tab. We will return to the other tabs when we look at files and folders in Chapter 7.

The **Windows Desktop Update** section is basically concerned with how the computer should respond to mouse clicks.

■ Select **Web style** or **Classic style** and click **Apply**.

This sets basic style for the Desktop. You can now tweak it to suit.

■ Select **Custom** and click **Settings...**

In the **Active Desktop** section, selecting **Enable all web-related content** is the same as turning on the **View as a web page** option (see page 17), and the **Customize** button takes you back to the **Customize Desktop** panel.

Ignore the two sets of **folder** options for the moment. We'll return to those when we look at files and folders (Chapter 7).

In the **Click items...** section, set how you want the computer to respond to single and double-clicks. The best settings are probably:

■ **Open with a single click** if you are a new user – it's simpler. You may want to set it so that you only get underlining when you point at an item – having everything underlined is messy.

■ **Double-click to open** if you have previously used earlier versions of Windows – it's the familiar way of working.

Experiment with the variations here, to see which suit you best. But once you have decided, stick with it! If you keep changing the effects of single and double-clicking, you will confuse yourself.

■ When you have set your options, click **OK** to close the **Settings** panel, and again to close the **Folder Options**.

2.4 Display Properties

The **Customize my Desktop** routine is the first stage of getting the screen the way you want it. Now let's turn to some other aspects of the Display Properties panel. Open it again.

■ Right-click on the Desktop to get the context menu, but this time select **Properties**. This time the panel will open with the **Background** tab at the front.

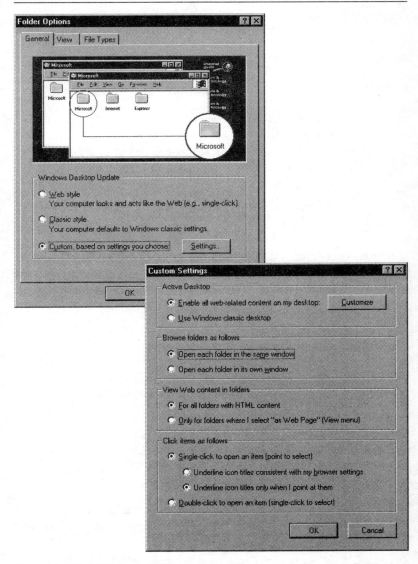

Figure 2.4 The **Custom Settings** dialog is reached from the **Settings...** button on the **Folder Options** panel. The **Customize...** button takes you back to the **Web** tab of the **Desktop Properties** panel.

The Background

This is purely decorative! The background can be a plain colour, a single picture, a small image 'tiled' to fill the whole screen or an HTML page (see opposite). Windows 98 has a selection of images (and one HTML page), but any JPG, GIF or BMP image or HTML page can be used.

1 Scroll through the list of images and pages. If you find one that sounds interesting, select it and it will be shown in the preview screen.

■ With a small image, set the **Display** mode to **Tile**. The image will be repeated across and down to fill the screen.

■ With a larger image, set the **Display** mode to **Center** to see it in its natural size, or **Stretch** to make it fill the screen.

2 Click **Apply** to test the choice. If you don't like it, try another.

3 Click **OK** to fix the choice and close the panel.

If, at some later point, you find an image – perhaps while surfing the Web – that you would like to use as your Desktop's 'wallpaper', save it, then reopen this panel and use the **Browse** button to set it as your background.

Some images can be set to Stretch or Tile!

Use **Browse** to find files elsewhere in your system.

Pattern applies to the area behind the text of icons. It can only be used when the Wallpaper is set to **None** – i.e. single colour background.

Figure 2.5 The **Background** tab.

HTML

HyperText Markup Language is the system used to create pages for the World Wide Web. It can display formatted text, images and multimedia files, as well as carrying links to other places on the Web or within your own computer or local network. HTML is easy to learn, but if you want a really simple way to create HTML pages, have a look at FrontPage Express (it's on the Windows 98 CD). If you want to learn HTML, try *Teach Yourself HTML*.

The Screen Saver

This is mainly decorative. A screen saver is a moving image that takes over the screen if the computer is left unattended for a while. On older monitors this prevented a static image from burning a permanent ghost image into the screen. Newer monitors do not suffer from this, but screen savers are more interesting than a static image on an idle screen.

The Settings options let you set the speed, colour, text or other features, depending on the choice of Screen Saver.

How long does the computer have to be idle before the Screen Saver should kick in?

Figure 2.6 The **Screen Saver** tab.

PROTECT FROM PRYING EYES

The Screen Saver can be password protected, so that it will hide the working screen until someone enters the correct password. This can be useful if you may not want passers-by to read your screen while you are away from your desk.

Appearance

Use this panel to set the colour and fonts for the Desktop and standard Windows-elements in all applications – the menus, dialog boxes, etc. You can select from a wide range of ready-made colour schemes, or adjust the settings for individual elements.

Some of the colour schemes are miracles of bad taste, others refined and easy on the eye. There are also a number of high contrast schemes, some with large fonts, for greater visibility. Experiment and find one you like.

Select an item by clicking on the screen or picking from the **Item** list, if you want to change its font, size or colour.

Figure 2.7 The **Appearance** tab. Click **Apply** to test a choice before you fix it and close the panel with **OK**.

Figure 2.8 One of the **High Contrast schemes**. For maximum visibility, try the High Contrast White, with extra large fonts. The Taskbar has been dragged to the side, but would normally be at the bottom.

Effects

Here you can change the images used for the Desktop icons, if you like – though the choice is limited unless you have bought the Plus pack of Windows 98 add-ons.

In the Visual Effects section, turn on **Use large icons** if you need the extra visibility. The other options are purely decorative, and can slow things down slightly as they all create more work for the system.

Settings

The Settings relate to the size of the screen and number of colours used in the display. They should normally be left alone as Windows 98 will select the optimum settings for your system – and the Advanced settings should certainly be left at their defaults unless you know and understand the details of your system. Bad selections here can really mess up your screen!

Figure 2.9 The **Effects** tab. If you also work on other computers, or other people also use yours, do not change the icons – it will cause confusion.

Figure 2.10 The **Settings** tab. The Screen area is set to the minimum here as this works better for the (small) pictures I need for this book. It is best set as large as your monitor can manage.

2.5 Summary

- The Desktop can be run in Web or Classic mode.
- If you want to link to the Internet through the Channels or other Active Desktop elements, as part of your normal working approach, use Web page mode.
- The Folder Options mainly control the way that the computer responds to the mouse. Once you have decided on your settings, stick with them to avoid confusion.
- Many aspects of the screen can be controlled through the Display properties panel.
- The Background, Screen Saver and Effects options are largely decorative and have little impact on the working of your system.
- The Appearance options can be set to high contrast and large fonts if you need to make the display easier to see.

3 | WORKING WITH WINDOWS

3.1 Aims of this chapter

If you only ever use one application at a time, you don't have to think too much about managing your windows – there will only be the one. But if you only ever use one application at a time, you are not really taking much advantage of Windows 98, a very effective multi-tasking system. If you want to have several applications open, you must know how to switch easily between them, and be able to arrange their windows so that you can work efficiently. This chapter will show you how.

HOW MANY WINDOWS AT ONCE?

There is no fixed limit to the number of windows that you can have open at the same time. The maximum depends on the amount of RAM memory on the computer and how memory-hungry the applications are. You won't run many big programs at once in a 16Mb machine, but 64Mb should be able to handle far more than you could ever realistically want.

I once had 30 applications running simultaneously, though 26 of these were started accidentally! (Don't lean on the **Enter** key when a application icon is selected on the Desktop...)

3.2 Basic windows concepts

A window is a framed area of the screen that exists and is controlled independently of any other windows. All applications are displayed in windows. If an application can handle multiple documents, each document is displayed in its own window within the application.

All windows have these features:

- **Title bar** along the top – showing the name of the application or document;
- **Minimize**, **Maximize/Restore** and **Close** buttons on the far right of the title bar – for changing the mode (page 28) and for shutting down;
- An icon at the far left of the Title Bar – leading to the window's **Control menu** (page 28);
- **Scroll bars** along the right and bottom – for moving the contents within the frame. These are only present if the contents are too wide or too long to fit within the frame.
- A thin outer **border** – for changing the size (see page 33).

Figure 3.1 The main features of windows. Notice that the icon and buttons are present in the Minimized document window – the one currently selected – and not in the other.

Application windows also have:

- **Menu bar** – giving access to the full range of commands and options;

- One or more **Toolbars** – containing icons that call up the more commonly-used commands and options. Toolbars are normally along the top of the working area, but may be down either side, or as 'floating' panels anywhere on screen.

- The **Status bar** – displaying a variety of information about the current activity in the application.

Both application and document windows can be in one of three modes, and the simplest way to switch them is with the buttons at the top right:

- **Maximize** – An application window fills the screen and loses its outer frame. When a document is Maximized in its application's working area, its Title Bar is merged with the application Title Bar and its Window Control button are placed on the far right of the Menu Bar.

- **Restore** – the window is smaller than the full screen or working area. Its size can be adjusted, and it can be moved to any position – within or beyond the limits of the screen.

- **Minimize** – an application is then visible only as a button on the Taskbar. A Minimized document is reduced so that only the Title Bar and Window mode buttons are visible.

Maximize and **Restore** are different faces of the same button.

The Control menu

This is opened by clicking the icon at the far left of the Title bar. But this is really here for keyboard users.

Press **Alt** and the **Space bar** to open the menu in applications, or **Alt** and the **Minus** key in documents.

You can now Minimize, Maximize/Restore or Close using the keys. (Notice that **Alt + F4** is a shortcut for Close.)

This is also where keyboard users start to Move (page 36) or change the Size (page 33) of the window.

Figure 3.2 When the document window is Maximized, its Title bar disappears. The document name is incorporated into the application Title bar; the document Control menu icon and buttons are placed in the Menu bar.

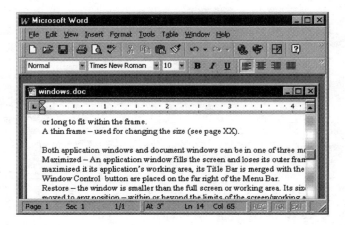

Figure 3.3 A window can be moved beyond the limits of the visible screen or of an application's working area. Fortunately it never completely disappears, so there is always something to grab hold of to drag it back into view (see page 36).

3.3 Using the Scroll bars

When you are working on a large picture or a long document, only the part that you are working on will be displayed within the window. Scroll bars will be present along the bottom and/or right of the frame and can be used to move the hidden parts of the document into the working area. They can be controlled in three ways:

- Click on the arrows at the ends to nudge the contents in the direction of the arrow – typically the movement will be a line or so at a time, but the amount of movement varies with the application and document size.
- Click on the bar to the side of or above or below the slider for a larger movement – typically just less than the height or width of the working area.
- Drag the slider. This is the quickest way to scroll through a large document.

Small movement

Large movement

Slider – drag as needed

AUTOMATIC SCROLLING

If the typing, drawing or other movements that you make while working on your document take the current position out of the visible area, the document will be scrolled automatically to bring the current position back into view.

3.4 Screen layouts

Windows 98 allows you enormous flexibility in your screen layouts, though the simplest layout that will do the job is usually the best. You can only ever work on one application at a time – though you can copy or move files or data between two windows and there may be continuing activities, such as printing or downloading, going on in other windows. If you do not

actually need to see what is happening in the other windows, the simplest
layout is to run all applications in Maximized mode. The one that you are
working on will fill the screen, obscuring the others, but you can easily
bring one of those to the front by clicking on its button in the Taskbar.

THE WINDOWS KEY AND THE TASKBAR BUTTONS

If you don't want to or cannot use the mouse to click the
Taskbar buttons, hold down the **Windows** key and press **Tab**.
This will select one of the Taskbar buttons – keep pressing **Tab**
to move between the buttons. When the one you want is
selected, press **Enter** to activate its window.

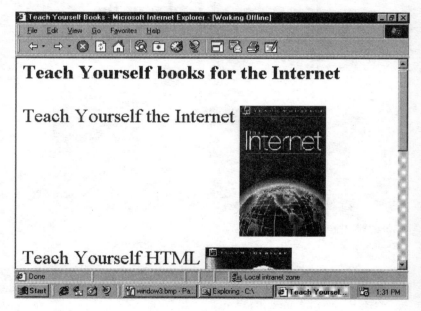

Figure 3.4 If you are only working on one application, you may as
well run it in a Maximized window and have the largest working/
viewing area. Other windows can be reached, when needed,
through their Taskbar buttons.

Multiple window layouts

Sometimes you will want to be able to see two or more windows at the same time – perhaps to copy material from one application to another or to copy or move files. The simplest approach here is to use the **Cascade** and **Tile** commands. They will take all windows currently open in Maximized or Restore mode and arrange them overlapping (**Cascade**), side-by-side (**Tile Horizontally**) or one above the other (**Tile Vertically**)

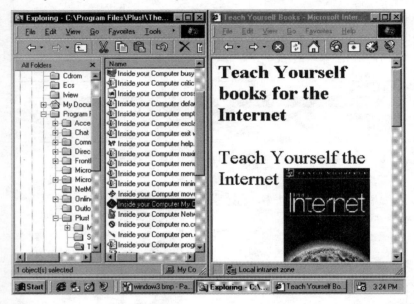

Figure 3.5 The **Tile** displays work better with bigger screens. A 640 x 480 can just cope with two windows, but no more.

- Check that all the windows you want to include in the display are in Maximized or Restore mode.
- Right-click on a blank area of the Taskbar.

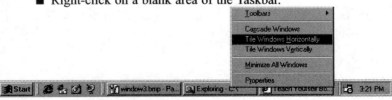

- Select the **Cascade** or **Tile Horizontally/Vertically** command.
- When you want to return to the previous layout, right-click the Taskbar again. The menu will now have an **Undo Cascade** or **Undo Tile** command.

3.5 Tabbing between windows

Switching between windows by using their Taskbar buttons is not always convenient. However, there are a couple of neat alternatives. This is the one I prefer:

- Hold down the **Alt** key and press **Tab**. This panel appears.

- Press **Tab** again until the application that you want is highlighted – if you go off the end, it cycles back to the start.
- Release the **Alt** key.

The second alternative is to hold **Alt** and press **Escape**. That also switches between windows and can be repeated until the right one is at the front of the Desktop.

3.6 Adjusting the window size

When a window is in Restore mode, its size can be adjusted freely. This can be done easily with the mouse or – less easily – with the keyboard.

Using the mouse

- Select the document or application window.
- Point to an edge or corner of the frame – when you are in a suitable place the cursor changes to a double-headed arrow.
- Hold down the left mouse button and drag the edge or corner to change the window size. If you have turned on the **Show windows contents while dragging** option (on the Effects

tab of the Display Properties, see page 23), the window will change size as you drag. If the option is off, you will see a shaded outline showing the new window size.

■ Release the mouse button.

■ Repeat on other edges or corners if necessary.

Using the keyboard

■ Open the Control menu by pressing **Alt + Space bar** (application) or **Alt + minus** (document).

■ Press **S** to select Size.

■ Press the arrow key corresponding to the edge that you want to move. A double-headed arrow will appear on that edge.

■ Use the arrow keys to move the edge into its new position.

■ Press **Enter** to fix the new size.

■ Repeat for other edges or corners if necessary.

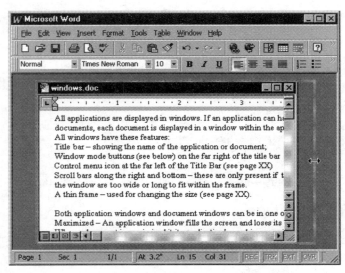

Figure 3.6 Adjusting the size of a document window. An outline shows the new size as the *Show windows contents while dragging* option has been turned off.

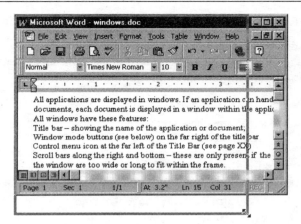

Figure 3.7 Adjusting the size by dragging on a corner – a more efficient way to change the size, though it can be trickier to locate the cursor at the start.

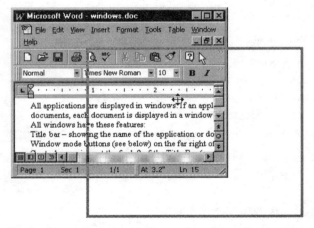

Figure 3.8 Moving a window. The 4-way arrow only appears when you start from the **Move** command in the Control menu. If *Show windows contents while dragging* is turned off, only the outline moves while you drag – the window then leaps into place when you release the mouse button.

3.7 Moving windows

A window in Restore mode can be moved to anywhere on – or part-ways
off – the screen (or the working area in an application). The Title bar is
the 'handle' for movement.

Moving with the mouse

■ Point to anywhere on the Title bar and drag the window into
its new place.

Moving with the keyboard

■ Open the Control menu and select **Move**.
■ Use the arrow keys to move the window as required
■ Press **Enter** to fix the new position.

3.8 Closing windows

When you have finished with a window, close it. This will free up memory
so that other applications run more smoothly, as well as reducing the clutter
on your Desktop.

There are three methods which will work with any window:

■ Click the **Close** button ☒ in the top right
corner.
■ Hold down **Alt** and press the **minus** key to
open the Control menu and select **Close**.
■ Hold down the **Alt** key and press **F4**.

You can also close a window by exiting from an application (see *Closing
programs*, page 56).

3.9 Shut Down

When you have finished a working session, you must shut down the system
properly – *do not simply turn off your PC*. Windows 98 runs through a
shutdown routine that removes any temporary files that were created by
the system or by applications, checks the system and closes down safely.
If you simply switch off, you may well find that it takes longer than usual

to restart, as Windows 98 will need to check – and possibly restore – essential system files. It may even insist on starting in 'Safe mode' and perform a thorough check there before allowing you to start up properly.

To shut down Windows 98:

1 Click **Start** and select **Shut Down**. If any windows are open, they will be closed, and you may be prompted to save documents (page 56).

or

Hold down the **Alt** key and press **F4** – if a window is open, it will close that, and you will have to press **Alt + F4** again to shut down.

2 Select **Shut down**.

3 Wait until you are told that it is safe before turning off your computer – it won't be long.

Alternative endings

■ Some newer PCs have a **Suspend** or **Hibernate** mode which shuts down the screen and hard drive, but leaves the memory intact. While suspended, the power consumption is virtually nil, but the computer can be restarted almost instantly. This is an attractive alternative to a full shut down.

■ If you have had a crash, **Restart** will normally restore order, though on very rare occasions you may need a full shut down and power-off to recover. (See page 56 for more on this.)

■ If you have an old MS-DOS program that cannot be run through the MS-DOS prompt – you can restart in MS-DOS mode.

■ If you are on a network, you can use the Start menu option to log off, leaving the computer ready for the next user.

3.10 Summary

■ Windows can be open in Maximized, Restore or Minimized modes.

■ To switch between the display modes, use the control buttons on the top right of the frame, or the commands on the Control menu.

■ If the contents of a window go beyond the boundaries of the frame, the Scroll bars can be used to pull distant areas into view.

■ There are many different ways to arrange windows on your screen – the simplest is to work with all windows Maximized, pulling them to the front as needed.

■ The Cascade and Tile arrangements will display all Maximized and Restore mode windows.

■ The size of a window can be changed by dragging on an edge or corner, or using the Control menu Size command and the arrow keys.

■ Windows can be moved by dragging on their Title bar, or with the Control menu Move command.

■ You must shut down Windows properly at the end of a session.

4 | HELP!

4.1 Aims of this chapter

If you ever get stuck while using Windows 98, there's plenty of help at hand. The Help system is comprehensive and well-indexed, with lots of cross-referencing and linking. As a result, when you need help, you should normally find it almost immediately or after a few moments' working through the system.

In addition to the main Help system, extra assistance is available in the form of brief tips, prompts and definitions, and there are Wizards to steer you through some of the trickier operations.

In this chapter you will learn how to get into the Help system and navigate through it to find the help that you need. You will also see how to make good use of the other forms of Help that Windows 98 offers.

4.2 Starting Help

The main Windows 98 Help system is reached through the Help item on the Start menu.

■ Click **Start**, select **Help** and you are in.

The utilities and applications that are supplied as part of Windows 98 – and most other Windows software, whether purchased or downloaded from the Internet – also have their own Help systems. New software, written to the Windows 98 standard, should be organised in the same way. The Help systems of older software may differ slightly, but will be similar enough, so that once you have mastered the main Windows 98 system you should be able to use the Help in any software.

Look at the Menu bar in any application and you will
see **Help** on the right. In the latest software, the first
item on this menu will be **Help Topics**; in older software,
the first will probably be **Contents** or **Contents and
Index**. Whatever the label, the first item is the way into the Help system.

F1 HELP

You can also start Help for Windows 98, or within any
application, by pressing F1 .

4.3 Contents

The Help system can be thought of as a book, with a different topic on
every page – though, unlike paper books, the pages very in length. Related
topics are arranged into chapters, and the whole book is extensively
indexed. But this is a reference book. Don't attempt to read it all from start
to finish, you'll just give yourself a headache.

The Help system normally opens at the **Contents** tab – if another tab is at
the front, click on the **Contents** label to switch to it. Use this tab to get an
overview of the available help, and when you want to read around a topic.
Initially, only the main section names will be visible.

- Beside each section name is a ▇ icon. Click on the section
  name or the icon to open the section.
- Some sections have subsections. Again, click on the name
  or ▇ to open one.
- When you see a list of topic pages, click on the name or [?]
  icon to display a page in the right-hand panel of the window.
- Only one section is open at a time – the open one will close
  when you select another. If you want to close a section so
  that you can reach those that are off-screen, click the ▇ icon.
- As you browse through the system, the **Back** and **Forwards**
  buttons become active, allowing you to return to pages that you
  have opened earlier in that session.

The Help pages contain descriptions of what things are and how they work,
with instructions on how to perform tasks. The pages (in Windows 98 and

in the latest applications) are written in HTML – HyperText Markup Language – the same coding system that is used for creating Web pages.

You will find that some text is underlined and hyperlinked – point to it and the cursor changes to 🖐. Click and one of three things will happen:

- If the text is **Click here to...** a Wizard or application will start.
- If the text is **Related Topics**, either you will be shown a list of relevant pages from which you can pick one, or you will be taken directly to the related page if only one is available.

Switch to the Contents tab
Revisit pages opened earlier
Open the section
Display the page
Close the section
You may have a choice of Related Topics

Figure 4.1 Windows **Help** system with the **Contents** tab in use. It's worth remembering that the window can be Maximized for ease of reading, or resized and moved so that you can see the problem while you are reading the Help.

■ If the text is a <u>special term</u>, a panel will appear giving an definition of the term. Click anywhere to close the panel.

4.4 Index

The **Contents** tab is good for browsing, but when you want to find out about a specific topic, you will find it faster through the **Index** tab. This contains an alphabetical list of entries, with subentries. Use it much as you would use the index of a book – by looking for *keywords*. (And a keyword is simply one which best describes the material you want to find, or that you could expect to find on a page about that topic.)

■ In the text box at the top type the first letter of the keyword. The list will scroll to bring into view the first word that starts with that letter.

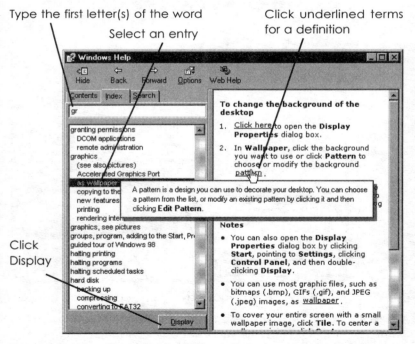

Figure 4.2 Using the **Index** tab. No matter where you start from, you reach the same set of Help pages.

- If the word you want is not yet visible, type more letters.
- Select an entry or subentry from the list and click
- If the reference leads to several Help pages, you will be presented with a Topics Found list – select one from here and click Display .

CREATING THE INDEX

The first time that you use the Index, you will have to wait for a moment while the system scans the Help pages to create it.

4.5 Search

At first glance this might seem to do pretty much the same job as the Index tab – both use keywords to find pages – but there is a crucial difference between them. The Index is created from selected words and phrases, and the entries are grouped by topic. In contrast, the Search is based on a full-text search of all the Help pages. As a result, the Search will find all pages that contain any given word, while the Index will only give you those that had merited an index entry.

Use the Search for:

- Finding words that are not in the Index
- Tracking down further references, after you have worked through the main pages, found through the Index.

To perform a search:

- Switch to the Search tab.
- Type the keyword – in full – into the text box.
- Press **Enter** or click List Topics .
- Select a Topic from the list and click Display .

Switch to the Search tab

Type the keyword

Click List topics

Select a Topic

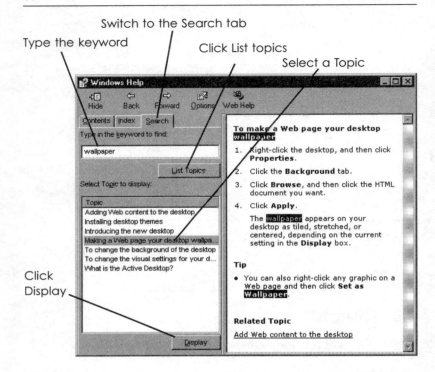

Click Display

Figure 4.3 Using the **Search** tab. The keyword is normally highlighted wherever it occurs in the page (but see *Tools and options* below).

4.6 Tools and options

The Help system has a small set of tools and options, which should give you all the control you need – most of the time you will probably go into Help, find and read a page or two, and come straight out again.

 Shuts the tab area, leaving just the page display – use it if you want to see more of the window beneath while you read the Help. The icon then changes to Show – click this when you want to restore the tabs to view.

 Reopens the Help page opened before the current one (if any) during the session.

Figure 4.4 If you want to be able to see more of the screen beneath while you are reading the Help pages, hide the tabs, and resize the window.

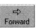 Used after a **Back** move, to return to the next Help page in the sequence of those opened during the session.

 Half of these duplicate the tools. Of the rest, these are worth noting:

Refresh If you click on an underlined term for the definition, or resize the window, the screen does not always redisplay correctly afterwards. Use Refresh to tidy it up.

Print Sends the current page to the printers

Highlighting On/Off Controls the highlighting of matching words in the Search displays.

 If you are online, this will connect to the Microsoft site where you can get help with more advanced features or with technical problems. We will return to this when we look at the Internet in Chapter 10.

4.7 Tips and prompts

There are lots of little – but handy – bits of Help available in Windows 98.

Tooltips

The icons on tool buttons are generally good *reminders* of the nature of the tool, but they are not always immediately obvious to the new user. These pop-up labels to tell you what tool icons stand for.

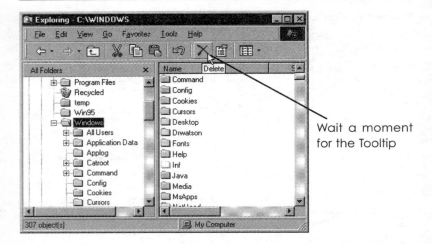

Figure 4.5 If you don't know what an icon does, point to it and wait a second. A 'tooltip' will appear, giving its name. If you still need help with the tool, at least you now know what to look up in the Index.

Figure 4.6 When you point to an entry in the menu system, a brief description appears in the Status bar at the bottom of the window.

Status bar prompts

The Status bar serves many purposes – it is through here that applications will communicate with you, so do keep an eye on it. One of the uses is to display a brief description of items as you point to them in the menus.

Dialog box help

If you look in the top right corner of dialog boxes and panels, you will normally see a [?] button. You can use this to get explanations of the options, buttons and other features in the dialog box. Here's how:

1 Click [?]. The cursor changes to ☾?.
2 Click on the item that you do not understand. A panel will open, displaying an explanation of the item.
3 Click again – anywhere – to close the explanation panel.

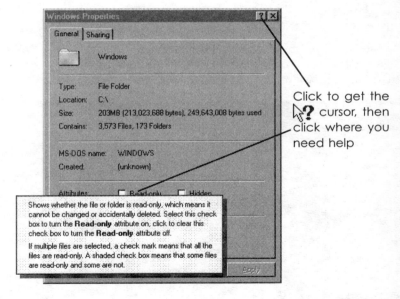

Click to get the ☾? cursor, then click where you need help

Figure 4.7 When you first use a new dialog box, it's good to be able to get explanations of its options and features.

4.8 Wizards

The Wizards are not part of the Help system, but they play an important role in making Windows 98 easy to use. As a general rule, if you have hardware or software to set up or reconfigure – especially if it is a lengthy or tricky operation – there will be a Wizard to help you through it.

All Wizards run in much the same way. You will see a series of panels. Each will ask you to set an option or provide some information, and will give you guidance on how you should respond.

At the bottom of the panel are three buttons:

| < Back | Takes you back a step so that you can review or change options set at that stage. |

| Next > | Takes you on to the next panel. When you reach the final panel, this is replaced by Finish . |

| Cancel | Closes the Wizard, abandoning any settings you have made up to that point. |

That Cancel button is more useful than you might think. There will be times when you get part way through a Wizard and realise that you do not have the information that you need to complete the operation.

Figure 4.8 A typical panel from a Wizard – this one will help you to organise the routine maintenance on your computer. (For more on this, see Chapter 12.)

4.9 Summary

Windows 98 tries to be user-friendly and to provide help where it is needed.

- To get help with Windows 98, use the Help command on the Start menu.
- To get help in an application, use the Topics or Contents on the Help menu.
- You can browse the Help pages from the Contents tab.
- To find help on a specific topic, use the Index or Search tabs.
- Tooltips and Status bar prompts can help you to get to grips with the tools and commands in a new application.
- The ? icon will give you explanations of the features of dialog boxes and panels.
- There are Wizards to help you with most configuration tasks.

5 | PROGRAMS AND DOCUMENTS

5.1 Aims of this chapter

The whole purpose of Windows 98 is, of course, to run applications and produce documents – almost everything in the system is concerned directly or indirectly with doing this. So, it's about time that we had a look at how to run applications, and how applications and documents are interrelated.

5.2 Definitions

Let's start with some definitions.

Program

A program is a set of instructions, that make the computer perform a task. The task may be very simple, or highly complex. It is useful to divide programs into three types:

Operating system level programs

These are run and controlled by Windows 98 – which is itself a program (or rather a set of interlinked programs). You are only aware of them by their effect. They manage the screen, pick up your keystrokes and mouse movements, control the transfer of data to and from the disk drives, prepare documents for output to the printer, and similar chores. Those of us who cut our computing teeth on older operating systems sometimes regret that Windows 98 takes such total control of these, but overall it must be admitted that Windows 98 does a very good job of management.

Utilities

These are the ones that you use to manage your computer. Windows Explorer and My Computer, for example, allow you to organise the storage of files on your disks (see Chapter 7). There are a whole bunch of programs in the Control Panel (Chapter 8) which you can use to customise the hardware and software on your computer, and another set that will enable you to keep your disks in good order (see Chapter 12).

Applications

These are why you use computers. They include business applications such as word-processors, spreadsheets, databases and accounts packages; graphics software for creating and editing images; Web browsers and other tools for communicating and working co-operatively on the Internet and on local networks; multimedia viewers, players and editing software; games and much else. Most, though not all applications, will produce or display documents, and any given application can only handle documents of a certain type or range of types. We'll return to this after one last definition.

Document

A document is an organised set of information produced by an application. It can be stored on disk as a file and can – typically but not always – be output onto paper, to be read or viewed away from the computer. The most obvious examples of documents are letters, essays and reports created on word-processors, but databases, spreadsheets and Web pages are also documents, as are images, sound and video files.

When a document is saved, part of its name identifies the application that created it. This association with applications is central to the way that Windows 98 handles documents. We will return to it in section 5.8.

5.3 Start ➔ Programs

The simplest way to start an application or utility program is through the **Start** menu. Almost all of the programs currently on your computer, and of those that you install later (see page 96), should have an entry in the **Programs** section of the menu.

A program may be on the first level of this menu, or may have been grouped onto a submenu – which may open up to a further level of submenus. The routines that install Windows 98 and new software will create the Start menu entries and organise them into submenus, but if you do not like the structure, you can tailor it to suit yourself (see Chapter 9).

Figure 5.1 Starting a program from the Start menu. In this case, the program, **Phone Dialer**, was on the third level of submenus. Notice **Windows Explorer** on the top level menu – you'll be needing that shortly! Notice also the Desktop Shortcuts in the background. These give quick access to regularly-used programs and folders.

To start a program:

1 Click ▒▒Start or press 🎹 on your keyboard.
2 Point to **Programs**.
3 Click once on a program name.
or
4 Point to a group name to open the next level of menu – and again if necessary – then select from there.

5.4 Other ways to start

Explorer/My Computer

Windows Explorer and My Computer are the standard Windows 98 file and folder management applications. The two do the same job in very similar ways, with very similar screen displays. We will be looking closely at these in Chapter 6. At this point it is worth noting that programs can be started from within them.

1 Open the folder containing the program file.
2 Click (or double-click) on the program name to start it.

Figure 5.2 Programs can be run from **Explorer** or **My Computer**, though it may sometimes take a while to find them!

WHY START FROM EXPLORER OR MY COMPUTER?

Not all programs have Start menus entries. For example, when you download software from the Internet, it is often in the form of a self-extracting Zip file – compressed and stored in an executable file (i.e. a program). When this is run, it extracts the software and installs it on to your system, normally creating Start menu entries so that you can run the new software. But, that downloaded file will not have a menu entry. To run it, you will have to find it on your disk and run it through Explorer or My Computer.

Desktop Shortcuts

Shortcuts offer a quick route to regularly-used folders and programs. When you first start using Windows 98, you will find a dozen of these icons on the Desktop. Some, such as My Documents, lead to folders – click on these and My Computer (see Chapter 7) will run, open at the selected folder. Others, such as Internet Explorer, lead to applications – click on these to start the application.

Over time you may want to add more shortcuts to favourite applications. This can be done easily through either Explorer or My Computer (see Chapter 7).

Taskbar toolbars

Initially, there is only one of these on the Taskbar, and that is the Quick Launch Toolbar (page 5). It contains shortcuts to Internet Explorer, Outlook Express and Channels, as well as 🗗 Show Desktop, which sets all open windows to Minimize, clearing the Desktop. Other Toolbars can be added – you can even create your own if you like this way of starting applications (see Chapter 9).

Start Run

The first item on the main part of the Start menu is Run. Click on this and a small panel opens. Here you can type a command line to start a program.

The command line must include the path – the route from the drive through the folders and subfolders to reach the one containing the program, e.g. \WINDOWS\COMMAND\MEM.EXE. If the program is not on the C: drive, the line must start with the drive letter (A: for the floppy and D: or E: – for the CD-ROM).

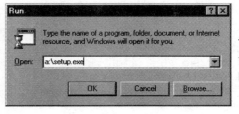

The **Run** panel being used to start an installation program from the A: drive.

There are two situations in which you may want to use the Run approach to starting a program:

- If you are installing new software from a floppy disk or CD-ROM, there will usually be an installation program (typically called SETUP.EXE). This can be started by typing the drive letter, then the path if necessary, followed by the program name, e.g. A:\SETUP.EXE.

  Remember that you can also use Explorer or My Computer to locate and start these installation programs.

- Some programs – particularly MS-DOS ones – have start-up options which you can set by typing them into the command line. If you ever come across such a program, the start-up options will be explained in a README file. It is not something which will concern most people.

5.5 Starting from documents

Every type of document is – or can be – linked to an application (see section 7.11, *File Types*), so that any time you open a document, Windows will run the appropriate application for you. Those documents that you have been working on recently can be opened from the Documents folder on the Start menu:

1 Click on **Start**.

2 Point to **Documents**. Its submenu contains shortcuts to your most recently used documents.

3 Select one to run the linked application and open the document.

- Documents can also be opened from Windows Explorer or My Computer (See Chapter 7).

DOCUMENTS FROM THE WEB

Internet Explorer also uses the File Types links – if it meets a file that it cannot handle, it opens the linked application to display the document (see Chapter 10).

5.6 Closing programs

When you have finished using an application, it
must be closed down properly. Closing its window
(page 36) will close the program, but you will also
find a Close or Exit option on the File menu.

If you have created a new file or edited an old one,
and not saved the changes, you will be prompted to
save before the application closes.

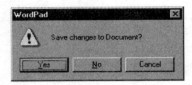

- Select **Yes** to save the file.
- Select **No** to exit without saving.
- Select **Cancel** to return to the application.

5.7 Coping with crashes

Windows 98 is more reliable and robust than earlier versions of Windows,
but software is rarely perfect. Some applications – and in particular some
combinations of applications – are more likely than others to crash. If you
are interested, crashes are normally caused by two programs trying to use
the same area of memory, and you can go find a big technical book if you
want to know more!

If you are lucky, you won't have crashes often. But just in case...

Symptoms

One or more of:

- The busy symbol ⧖ appears and stays (but do wait twice as
  long as normal just in case it has a lot more to do than you
  thought).
- No response to key presses or mouse actions.

- The screen does not display properly – there might be part of a window or dialog box left behind and unmovable.

Solution

- Hold down **Ctrl** and **Alt**, and press **Delete**. The **Close Programs** dialog box will appear, and the program that has crashed will be at the top of the list – with 'not responding' after the name.

Figure 5.3 The **Close Programs** dialog box. If the highlighted program is not marked 'not responding', it probably hasn't crashed – click **Cancel** and give Windows a bit longer to sort itself out.

- If it is an application that is not responding, click **End Task** – you will be asked to confirm that you really want to close it down. The system should work properly once it is out of the way.
- If *Explorer* or *Systray* is 'not responding', click **Shut Down**. These are core programs – Windows cannot function unless they are both working properly.

NEED MORE RAM?

If your system is light on memory and you are running several big applications, switching between them can be very slow as Windows parks the data from one into temporary storage on disk then reloads the data from the other – it might appear to have crashed. You can work with 16Mb, but 32Mb is a more realistic minimum if you want to run, say, two Office applications and a few smaller programs at the same time.

5.8 Filenames and extensions

When documents are saved onto disk, they are given a name which has two parts. The first part identifies that particular document, and can be more or less anything you want (see *Rules for Filenames*, below). The second part is a three-letter extension which identifies the type of document. This is normally set by the application in which the document is created, and it is through this extension that Windows 98 can link documents and applications. (We'll look at how to create these links in Chapter 7.)

Here are some extensions that you are likely to meet:

.TXT	Simple text, e.g. from NotePad
.DOC	Word document
.WB1	Excel WorkBook (spreadsheet)
.HTM	Web page – can be created by many applications
.BMP	bitmap image, e.g. from Paint
.GIF	a standard format for image on Web pages
.JPG	an alternative format for Web page images
.WAV	audio file in Wave format
.EXE	an executable program – not a document!

Rules for filenames

The first part of the name can be as long as you like (up to 250 characters!) and can consist of any combination of letters, numbers, spaces and underlines, but no other symbols. It's common sense to make sure that the name means something to you, so that you can easily identify the file when you come back to it later – and the shorter the name, the smaller the chance of making a mistake if you have to type it again.

The extension must match the application. As a general rule, when you save a file for the first time, simply give the identifying name and let the application set the extension. If the application can output documents in different formats, and you know that you need a particular format, select it from the **Save as type** list. After the first save, the filename is set, though the file could be later saved under a different name and in a different format. You might, for example, have written a report in Word, but want to give a copy to a colleague who used WordPerfect.

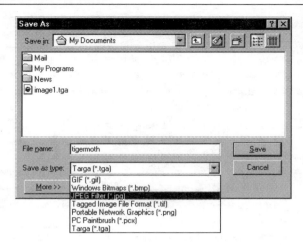

Figure 5.4 A typical **Save As** dialog box. This one is from a graphics package, and can save in several standard formats. Many applications can handle documents in their own 'native' format and import or export them in other formats.

STANDARD FORMATS

Life would be easier if there was only one standard format for each type of document, but instead there are loads of them, especially for word-processing and graphics. You might wonder why. According to the old joke, computer people love standards which is why they have so many.

In fact, there are several reasons. When a software house develops a new application, or a new version of an existing one, it will normally use a different document format – partly to handle its special features, and partly to distinguish it from its rivals. Some formats are developed to meet particular needs. With graphics documents, for instance, there is a trade-off between file size and image quality, and formats have been developed across the range.

5.9 Summary

- There are three main types of programs: those run by the operating system, utilities for managing your computer, and applications for doing useful work or having fun!

- The data files produced by or displayed by applications are known as documents.

- Programs can be set running from the Start menu, Desktop Shortcuts, the Taskbar, the Run dialog box or from within Explorer or My Computer.

- Opening a document in the Start Documents menu or in Explorer or My Computer will run its associated application.

- Programs should be closed down properly when you have finished using them.

- If a program crashes and hangs the system, the **Ctrl** + **Alt** + **Delete** key combination will open the Close Programs dialog box. You should be able to close the offending program from here.

- Documents are given filenames when they are saved onto disk. These have two parts: the first part is simply an identifying name and can be more or less anything you like; the second part describes the format of the file and is usually set by the application in which it was created.

6 | BASIC TECHNIQUES

6.1 Aims of this chapter

One of the great attractions of Windows is consistency. Every Windows application will have a similar basic layout and tackle the same jobs in much the same ways. As a result, once you have learnt how to use one application, you are well on the way to knowing how to use any other Windows applications. This chapter looks at some of the basic techniques for working with Windows – selecting objects, moving objects on screen and copying through the Clipboard and through scraps.

6.2 Selection techniques

Before you can do any work on an object or a set of objects – e.g. format a block of text, copy part of an image, move a group of files from one folder to another – you must select it.

Text

Use WordPad, NotePad or any word-processor to try out these techniques. They can also be used with text objects in graphics packages and even with small items of text such as filenames.

With the mouse:
1 Point to the start of the text.
2 Hold down the left mouse button and drag across the screen.
3 The selected text will be highlighted.

With the keyboard:
1 Move the cursor to the start of the text.
2 Hold down the **Shift** key.
3 Use the arrow keys to highlight the text you want.

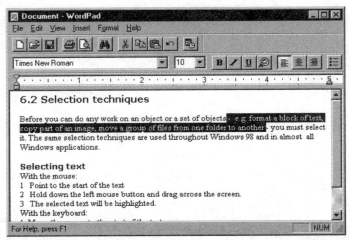

Figure 6.1 Once the text has been selected, it can be formatted, deleted, copied or moved.

Graphics

The same techniques are used for images in graphics applications, and for icons on the Desktop, files in Explorer (Chapter 7) and other screen objects.

Single object:

   1 Point to it. If this does not highlight it, click on it.

Adjacent objects

   1 Imagine a rectangle that will enclose the objects.

   2 Point to one corner of this rectangle.

   3 Hold down the left mouse button and drag across to the opposite corner – an outline will appear as you do this.

   or

   2 Select the object at one corner.

   3 Hold down **Shift** and select the object at the opposite corner.

Scattered objects:

   1 Highlight the first object.

   2 Hold down the **Ctrl** key and highlight each object in turn.

   3 If you select an object by mistake, point to (or click on) it again to remove the highlighting.

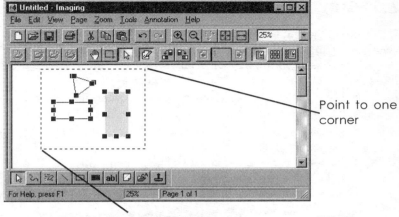

Point to one corner

Drag to the opposite corner

Figure 6.2 Selecting images and other objects.

DELETING OBJECTS

All applications have a Delete command (usually on the Edit menu), but selected objects can also be deleted by pressing

 Delete or ⬅ . Use these with care!!

6.3 Cut, Copy and Paste

If you look at the Edit menu of any Windows application, you will find the commands **Cut**, **Copy** and **Paste**. You will also find them on the short menu that opens when you right-click on a selected object. These are used for copying and moving data within and between applications.

■ **Copy** copies a selected block of text, picture, file or other object into a special part of memory called the *Clipboard*.

■ **Cut** deletes selected data from the original application, but places a copy into the Clipboard.

■ **Paste** copies the data from the Clipboard into a different place in the same application, or into a different application – as long as this can handle data in that format.

Figure 6.3 The short menu offers the quickest route to the **Cut** and **Paste** commands. If the Clipboard is empty, Paste will be 'greyed out' or omitted from the menu.

The data normally remains in the Clipboard until new data is copied or cut into it, or until Windows is shut down. (Some applications have a **Clear Clipboard** command.) If you want to see what's in the Clipboard – just for interest, as this serves few practical purposes – you can use the Clipboard Viewer. It should be on the **Programs ➙ Accessories ➙ Systems Tools** menu. (This is an optional utility and may not have been installed.)

Figure 6.4 Pasting a copied image in **Paint**. Selected graphics usually have an enclosing frame with 'handles' at the corners and mid-sides. You can drag within the frame to move the object, or on the handles to resize it.

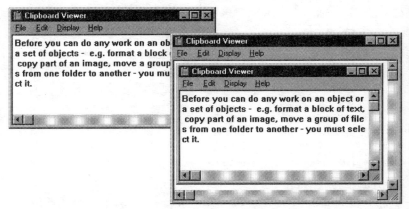

Figure 6.5 Two shots of the **Clipboard Viewer**. The first is after copying some text; the second is after capturing the screenshot of the Viewer – which is stored in the Clipboard! The Clipboard can hold data in any format, and the Viewer can display all major Windows formats.

6.4 Drag and drop

This is an alternative to Cut and Paste for moving objects within an application or between compatible applications. It is also the simplest way to rearrange files and folders in Windows Explorer, as you will see in the next chapter.

The technique is simple to explain:

1 Select the block of text or the object(s).
2 Point anywhere within the highlighted text or in the frame enclosing other objects.
3 Hold down the mouse button and drag the object across the screen or, with text, move the cursor (which is now 🔖).
4 Release the button to drop the object into its new position.

In practice, accurate positioning depends upon good mouse control. And one of the best ways to improve your mouse control is to play the games. The card games use drag-and-drop for moving cards; Minesweeper helps to build speed and accuracy. (Remember this when you need an excuse.)

Figure 6.6 Dragging text in **WordPad** – the display will be much the same in any word-processor. The target position for the text is indicated by the thin bar to the right of the arrow.

Figure 6.7 You can drag a document from **My Computer** or **Windows Explorer** and drop it into a suitable application – this is sometimes quicker than opening files from within the application.

6.5 Scraps

A scrap is typically a fragment of a word-processor document – though it could be the whole of one, parked on the Desktop. Scraps can be used as highly visible reminders of urgent jobs, or to hold blocks of text that you will reuse in other files, or simply as temporary storage.

What distinguishes a scrap from an ordinary file is the way that it is created and used.

1 Set the word-processor window into Restore mode so that some of the Desktop is visible.

2 Select the text.

3 Drag the selection and drop it on the Desktop.

4 To reuse the scrap, either drag it into the application window,

or Double-click on it to open the application and load in the scrap document.

Figure 6.8 Creating a scrap. To reuse it, drag it back into the application.

6.6 Summary

- Text can be selected either with the mouse or the keyboard.
- Graphics and other objects are selected by dragging an outline around them, or by using the mouse in conjunction with Shift or Ctrl.
- Selected data can be cut or copied to the Clipboard, then pasted into the same or a different application.
- The Clipboard Viewer can be used to see what's in the Clipboard.
- Text and some kinds of objects can be moved using drag and drop.
- Text can be stored on the Desktop as scraps.

7 | FILES AND FOLDERS

7.1 Aims of this chapter

If you want to be able to use your computer efficiently, you must know how to manage your files – how to find, copy, move, rename and delete them – and how to organise the folders on your disks. In Windows 98, these jobs can be done through either Windows Explorer or My Computer – the two are almost identical. In this chapter we will have at look at these utilities and see how they can be used for file and folder management. We will also look at creating links between documents and applications, through the File Types routine, and at the Recycle Bin – a neat device which makes it much less likely that you will delete files by accident.

7.2 Disks and folders

A floppy disk holds 1.4 Mb of data – enough space for a dozen or so decent-sized documents. A 'small' hard drive nowadays has 2 Gigabytes of storage – over 1,400 times as much as a floppy! Obviously, with this much storage space, it must be organised if you are ever to find anything.

The organisation comes through a structure of *folders*. A folder is an elastic-sided division of the disk. It can contain any number of files and subfolders – subfolders can contain other subfolders, and so on *ad infinitum*. The structure is often described as a tree. The *root* is at the drive level. The main folders branch off from here, and each may have a complex set of branches leading from it. At the simplest, a C: drive might contain three folders – *My Documents*, *Program Files* (which will have subfolders for each application) and *Windows* (which has subfolders for the sets of programs and files that make up the different parts of the Windows 98 system). As you will see in section 7.7, you can create new folders, rename them, delete them and move them to produce your own folder structure.

FLOPPY FOLDERS

Floppy disks can also be divided into folders, if you want to
keep several distinct sets of files on the one disk.

7.3 Windows Explorer

Windows Explorer, or Explorer for short,
is the key tool for managing your files and
folders. Get to know this program!

- To run it, click Start and point
  to Programs.
- Windows Explorer is always the
  bottom item on the Programs
  menu. Click once to run it.

When Explorer opens, it will display the contents of your C: drive – the
main (and perhaps the only) hard disk. The window has two panels.

The one on the left (the **Explorer Bar**) normally shows **All Folders**, though
this can be used for other things or closed if not wanted (see page 73). In
the folder display, ⊞ to the left shows that a folder contains subfolders.
Click on this to open up the branch. The icon changes to ⊟ – clicking this
will close the branch.

When a folder is selected 📂 in **All Folders**, its files and subfolders are
listed in the main pane. Files can be listed by name, type, date or size, and
displayed as large or small icons, with or without details (see page 76).

The **Status bar** at the bottom shows the number of objects in the folder
and the amount of memory they use, or the size of a selected file.

The controls

These are at the top of the window. The **Menu bar** is always visible. As
with any Windows application, the full command set can be reached through
the menu system, but those that you will use most often can be accessed
faster through toolbar buttons or keyboard shortcuts.

Note: The menu options vary slightly, when a file, folder or drive is selected.

Root   Top-level folders   Current folder   Subfolders

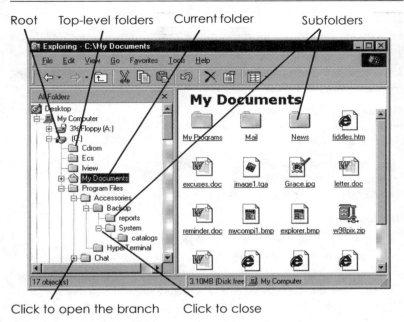

Click to open the branch   Click to close

Figure 7.1 Windows Explorer, showing the main features. Yours may well look different as there are many combinations of display options.

Back   Forwards   Up   Undo   Properties   Views

Figure 7.2 The **Standard toolbar**. Drop-down lists from the Back and Forwards buttons provide an easy way to move between folders that you have selected earlier in the same session.

There are three toolbars, all of which
are optional – turn them on or off
through the **View** menu.

The **Standard toolbar** (Figure 7.2)
contains buttons for all essential jobs.

The **Address Bar** shows the current
selected folder, and can be useful for
navigating around the system.

Links are shortcuts to places on the
Internet – yes, you can go there from
within Explorer (see Chapter 10).

The Standard buttons

(with **menu commands** and *keyboard shortcuts*)

- Back (**Go ➡ Back** *Alt+Left*) and Forward (**Go ➡ Forward**
  Alt+Right) Each time you select a folder, it is added to the
  lists that drop down from these buttons (and you have to go
  Back before you can go Forward).

- Up (**Go ➡ Up one level**) takes you to the next higher-level
  folder, or from a main folder to the drive, or from a drive up
  to My Computer.

- Cut (**Edit ➡ Cut** *Ctrl+X*) – deletes the selected file but keeps
  a copy in the Clipboard (see page 64).

- Copy (**Edit ➡ Copy** *Ctrl+C*) – copies the selected file to the
  Clipboard.

- Paste (**Edit ➡ Paste** *Ctrl+V*) – copies the file from the
  Clipboard into the current folder.

- Undo (**Edit ➡ Undo** *Ctrl+Z*) – undoes the previous action,
  if possible. In practice, about the only things that can be
  undone are some of the view options.

- Delete (**File ➡ Delete** *Delete*) – deletes the selected file or
  folder, placing it in the Recycle Bin (page 88).

- Properties (**File ➡ Properties**) – opens the Properties panel
  for the selected file or folder.

- Views – leads to a drop-down list containing the main options
  from the View menu.

Drag the handles up or down to move a toolbar,
left or right to resize it

Figure 7.3 The **Address bar** offers a quick way to get around your
system – especially if you have opened up several levels of branches,
producing a very long All Folders display.

7.4 View options

Explorer Bar

If you click on View to open the menu,
point to Explorer Bar and wait a moment,
this submenu will open.

All Folders is the default, displaying the
folder structure.

Select **Search**, **Favorites**, **History** or
Channels and Windows Explorer will, in
effect, turn into Internet Explorer (see
Chapter 10).

Select **None** and the bar will close.

View → as Web Page

This is the most significant option on the View menu, but for best effect should be used with the Explorer Bar set to **None**. The left side of the window is then used for displaying details of the file or folder that is currently selected (i.e., the one you are pointing at). With some types of files, e.g. HTML documents (a Web page), GIF, JPG or BMP image, a preview will then be generated and shown below the details.

Figure 7.4 In **Web page view**, the area to the left of the contents list is used to display details, and sometimes a preview of the selected document. (This does not apply if Explorer is running in a small window, especially if the Explorer Bar is open.) In the example above files and folders are shown in Details view, giving their size, type and date.

View → Folder options

We met the **Folder Options** panel earlier when looking at Display Properties (page 18). This time, we'll turn to the **View** tab. *Note that the options can be set separately for each folder.* Some of the options here really are just fine-tuning, and you can come back and play with these when you want to see what they do. The following are more significant:

Figure 7.5 The **View** tab of **Folder Options**. The settings can be different for each folder – which makes sense. You may well want more detail in folders that contain documents that in those that contain program or system files.

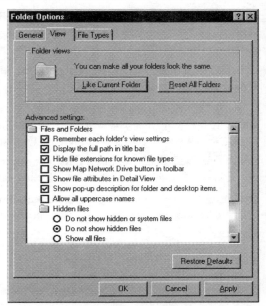

Folder views

Click **Like Current Folder** if you want the current settings to be applied to all folders. If you have got into a bit of a mess with your options (easily done!), click **Reset All Folders** to go back to the original settings.

Advanced Settings

Remember each folder's view settings will retain the separate options from one session to the next.

Hidden files – Windows 98 'hides' essential files, to prevent accidental deletion. They can be shown if you want to see them, or these and system files – also crucial – can be hidden. For safety, hide them.

Visual settings

When resizing and moving windows in Chapter 3 we noted that the window can be shown in outline only or its contents displayed during these operations. The **Show window contents while dragging** option can be turned on or off here.

7.5 Displaying and sorting files

Icons and Details

Files and folders can be shown as **Large icons**, **Small icons**, **List** or **Details** – make your choice from the **View** menu or from the drop-down list on the **Views** button.

Large icons aren't just easier to see, they are also larger targets if you are less than accurate with the mouse!

Small icons and **List** view differ only in the order – listing either across or down the screen. Both are good for selecting sets of files (see page 83).

Details gives a column display under the headings Name, Size, Type and Modified. Click on a heading to sort the files by that feature. Click a second time to reverse the sort order. This display is useful for tracking down files that you were working on at certain date (but have forgotten the names), or for finding old or large files if you need to create some space.

Click to sort on that column

Figure 7.6 The **Details** display allows you to sort the files easily.

ARRANGE ICONS

The **View → Arrange Icons** menu command can be used to sort the files by **Name**, **Type**, **Size** or **Date** in any mode, whether or not the details are displayed on screen.

7.6 My Computer

My Computer

My Computer can only be started from the Desktop icon. It is so similar to Windows Explorer that I'm not entirely sure why it's there at all! The Toolbars are identical, though the menus have a slightly smaller set of options. There is no Tools menu, so you cannot run a Find operation (page 90) from here. The Explorer Bar is normally closed and though you can run the Internet-based Search, Favorites, History and Channels here, there is no All Folders option. Apart from those few differences, the two utilities look and behave the same.

■ I find that Windows Explorer is better for general file and folder management as it gives you easy ways to switch from one folder to another, and to move files between folders.

Figure 7.7 My Computer, shown here in Web Page view, with large icons and the Address and Links toolbars turned off.

■ My Computer is convenient if you just want to work in one
   folder – to see or delete its contents.

If you set My Computer so that it opens a new window for every folder
(an option on the **Customs Settings** panel, see page 19), it can also be
used for reorganising your file storage.

Figure 7.8 Run My Computer in multiple windows if you want to move
files between the folders.

7.7 Organising folders

Windows 98 sets up one folder for your files, called *My Documents*. This
is unlikely to be enough for very long. You need to create more folders if:

■ you will be storing more than a few dozen documents – it's
   hard to find stuff in crowded folders;

■ more than one person uses the PC – everyone should have
   their own storage space;

■ your documents fall into distinct categories – personal,
   hobbies, different areas of work, etc.

Figure 7.9 Two approaches to a folder structure for someone who uses the PC for work and personal use. In the top one, the new folders have been created with *My Documents*; in the lower, the folders are all at the main level. Either works just as well.

MIXED CONTENTS

Putting documents of different types in one folder is not as confusing as it might seem. It might look untidy when you view it through Explorer – though sorting by Type will help to clarify. In practice, you will mainly access your documents through applications, and when you open a file there, the **Open File** dialog boxes will normally only list those of the right type.

Creating folders

A new folder can be created at any time, and at any point in the folder structure. Here's how:

1 In Explorer, select the folder which will contain the new one, or select the drive letter for a new top-level folder.

2 Open the **File** menu, point to **New** then select **Folder**.

Use File → New
→ Folder

Select the
containing
folder

3 Replace *New Folder* with a meaningful name.

Edit the name

■ If you decide the folder is in the wrong place, select it and
drag it into place in the All Folders list.

Folders can be
dragged to
rearrange the
structure – here
School is being
moved into
Roger's folder.

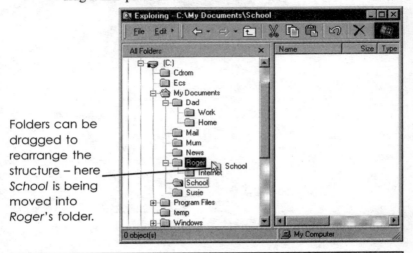

FOLDERS ARE FILES

We think of folders as containers, but to the PC they are files,
with lists of the names and disk locations of other files. They
are special – you cannot read them, and the system interprets
them to create the folder displays – but they can be renamed,
copied and deleted just the same as document files.

7.8 Creating shortcuts

A Desktop shortcut offers the simplest and quickest way to start an
application or open a folder – as long as you can see the Desktop! You can
create new ones in several ways. This is probably the easiest.

Application shortcuts

1 Open the application's folder in Explorer or My Computer.
2 Locate the program file. If you are not sure if it is the right
   one, click (or double-click) on it. If the application runs, it's
   the right file.
3 Drag the file onto the Desktop.

Figure 7.10 Creating a **Desktop shortcut** using Explorer.

    4 Edit the name to remove 'Shortcut to...', if you like.

Shortcuts to folders

    1 Select the folder in Explorer or My Computer.

    2 Hold the right mouse button down and drag the icon onto the Desktop.

    3 Select **Create Shortcut(s) Here**.

7.9 File management

Almost all of the document files in your system will come from one of two sources. You will create most of them yourself, working within applications. Some will have been downloaded from the Internet, or loaded in from commercial or friends' disks. This may be obvious, but the point is that files are rarely created within Explorer or My Computer – these are used for managing existing files. Even the **File → New** command merely opens the relevant application so that a file can be produced there.

Selecting files

Before you can do anything with your files, you must select them.

- ■ *To select a single file*, point to it (if you use the Web Page mode), or click once on it (in Classic mode).
- ■ *To select a set of adjacent files*, click on the window to the right of the top one and drag an outline over the set;

or select the first, hold down the **Shift** key, and select the last.

- ■ *To select scattered files*, select the first, hold down the **Control** key and select the rest in turn.

Hold **Control** to select
scattered files

Drag an outline
to highlight a set

Moving and copying files

Files are easily moved or copied. The technique is similar for both.

1 Select the file(s).

2 Scroll through the **All Folders** display and/or open subfolders, if necessary, until you can see the target folder.

3 Drag the file(s) across the screen until the target folder is highlighted, then drop it there.

- If the original and target folders are both on the same disk, this will move the selected file(s).
- If the folders are on different disks, or your target is a floppy disk, this will copy the file(s).

Drag the files to the target folder

If you want to move a file from one disk to another, or copy within the same disk, hold down the right mouse button while you drag. When you release the button, select **Move** or **Copy** from the short menu.

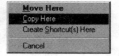

Cut, Copy and Paste

Files and folders can be copied and moved through the Clipboard (see page 64), just like any other objects in Windows 98. Dragging is generally simpler – but only in Explorer. If you are using My Computer, you can drag between multiple windows, or **Cut** and **Paste** in a single window.

Cut, **Copy** and **Paste** can be found on the **Edit** menu, or on the short menu that opens when you right-click on a file.

1 Select the file(s).

2 To move a file, click ![cut icon], or use the **Cut** command.

or to copy, click ![copy icon] or use **Copy**.

3 Go to the target folder and click ![paste icon] or use **Paste**.

- If you copy a file into the same folder, it will be renamed '*Copy of...*' (the original filename).

Renaming files

If you want to edit or retype a file's name, select the file and press **F2** on your keyboard, or use **Rename** from the **File** or shortcut menu. Change the name as required and press **Enter** to fix the new name.

- If you are working in Classic mode (where you click to select), a second click on the filename will switch into edit mode.

Select the file and use File → Rename

EXTENSIONS

When renaming files, do not change their extensions! If you do, you will lose the document–application link (page 88).

Sending files elsewhere

The **Send To** command on the File menu or the short menu offers a simple way to copy a file to a floppy disk, or to the Briefcase (Chapter 14), transfer it to your Mail system for sending by e-mail, or start to upload a Web page to your Web space. Just select the destination to begin!

Deleting files

If a file is no longer needed, select it and press **Delete** on your keyboard or use the **Delete** command. If you delete a folder, all its files are also deleted.

Windows 98 makes it very difficult to delete files by accident! First, you have to confirm – or cancel – the deletion at the prompt.

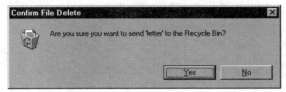

Second, nothing is permanently deleted at this stage. Instead, the file or folder is transferred to the Recycle Bin. Let's have a look at that now.

7.10 The Recycle Bin

The true value of the Recycle Bin is only appreciated by those of us who have used systems which lack this refinement, and have spent hours – or sometimes days – replacing files deleted in error! In practice, you will rarely need this, but when you do, you will be glad that it is there!

Figure 7.11 Files deleted in error can be restored from the Bin.

If you find that you need a deleted file, it can be restored easily.

Recycle Bin

1 Open the Recycle Bin, from the Desktop icon or from Windows Explorer (at the end of the All Folders list).

2 Select the file.

3 Open the **File** menu, or right-click for the short menu and select **Restore**.

■ If the file's folder has also been deleted, it will be re-created first, so that the file can go back where it came from.

One of the main reasons for deleting files is to free up disk space, but as long as they are in the Recycle Bin, they are still on the disk. So, make a habit of emptying the bin regularly. There is an **Empty...** option on the Bin's right-click menu, but this should only be used when you are absolutely sure that there is nothing in it that you might want to restore.

■ Play safe! Open the Bin and check its contents carefully, restoring any accidental deletions, before using the **File ➔ Empty Recycle Bin** command.

■ The default settings allows the Recycle Bin to use up to 10% of the drive's capacity, which should work well. If you want to change this, right-click on the Bin's icon to open its Properties panel and set the level there.

Figure 7.12 The Bin should be emptied regularly to free up disk space.

7.11 File Types

By now you should be familiar with the idea that documents can be associated with applications, through their File Types. It's time to have a closer look at this.

In Windows Explorer or My Computer, open the **View** menu and select **Folder Options...** At the Options panel, switch to the **File Types** tab. This lists all the 'registered' file types. There should be lots there already. Windows 98 sets up associations between a whole host of documents and applications when it first starts, and most applications will add their own types to the list as they are installed.

Select any one of them from the list, and in the bottom part of the panel you will see the **Extension**(s) that mark this type, the MIME type (used when documents are sent by e-mail) and the application that the document **Opens with**.

Figure 7.13 The **File Types** tab – scroll through the list. You will be amazed at how many types your system knows about already!

New File Types

Not all applications come equipped with the installation routines to set up associations for you – older software, and shareware downloaded from the Internet tend not to. If you want to be really thorough about it, you can go through all your applications, making a note of the file types that they can handle, then go through the File Types list and check that all are included. If any have been overlooked, you can create the association here, by clicking the **New Type** button. It's not a particularly difficult process – but it takes time, and there is an easier way to do things.

1 Close the File Types panel and forget about it.

2 When, at some point in the future, you try to open a document of an unregistered type, you will be presented with the **Open With** panel.

If you do not want to set up a permanent link with an application, clear this box and the document will be opened with the chosen program on this occasion only.

3 Scroll through the list of applications and select the right one for the type. If you cannot see it in the list, but know that it is on your system, click the **Other...** button and track down the program file.

4 If you want to give a description (to appear in the **File Types** list), do so, but this is not essential.

5 Click **OK**.

■ Now try to open the document and the associated application should run.

7.12 Find

Windows 98 has several Find utilities, but the one we are interested in here is **File or Folders**, which can track down lost files for you, hunting for them by name, location, contents, date, type and/or size.

If you organise your folders properly, and always store files in the right places, you'll never need this utility. However, if you are like me, you will appreciate it.

- In Explorer, open the **Tools** menu, point to **Find** and select **Files or Folders**.

or click **Start**, point to **Find** and select it there.

The **Find: All Files** panel has three tabs. Known details of the wanted files can be entered into any of these.

Name & Location

Use this tab if you can remember the filename, or any part of it. **Find** will look for any file (or folder) that contains the **Named** characters.

If you know that the file will be on a particular drive, or in a major folder, select this from the **Look in** drop-down list.

You can also base a
search on known
words in text files

Figure 7.14 Using the **Find** routine to track down the pictures for this chapter – I was concentrating on other things when I saved them.

Date

If you know when a file was created, modified or last accessed, you can
set the date limits. The little drop-down calendar provides a very neat way
to set dates!

Pick the option,
then set the
date limits

Previous month

Advanced

Here you can select the type of file from the drop-down list, and/or (less
usefully, I suspect) set the minimum or maximum file size.

DANGER! OVER-DEFINITION

When you start the search, Find will compare files against all
the details that you have entered on the three tabs. So, if you
try a Find based on one tab's details, e.g. the Name, and
that doesn't work, click **New Search** to clear all settings before
starting a new search.

7.13Summary

- Folders on hard (and floppy) disks create organised storage for your files.

- Windows Explorer is the main utility for managing files and folders. It has a comprehensive set of tools – the most useful of these can be reached through the toolbar buttons.

- The View options and Folder options allow you to set up the Explorer display to suit yourself.

- Files can be displayed as large or small icons, or in a detailed list. They can be sorted into name, size, type or date order.

- My Computer is a slightly simpler alternative to Explorer.

- You should create folders for each area of your computer work, and for each person who uses the machine. Folders can be created within other folders if needed.

- Desktop shortcuts can be created by dragging file or folder icons from Explorer or My Computer onto the Desktop.

- Files can be moved, copied, renamed or deleted as necessary.

- The Cut, Copy and Paste commands also work with files.

- To select sets of files, drag an outline with the mouse, or use the mouse in combination with Shift or Ctrl.

- When renaming files, do not change the extensions, as these identify the type of document.

- The Send command offers a simple way to copy a file to a floppy disk, or to e-mail it to someone.

- When a file is deleted, it is transferred to the Recycle Bin. If necessary, files can be restored from the Bin.

- The Recycle Bin should be emptied regularly to free up disk space.

- The simplest way to create a new File Types association is to select the appropriate application when Windows asks you what it should open a document with.

- The Find routine allows you to track down lost files through their name (or part of it!), location, date, type or size.

8 | THE CONTROL PANEL

8.1 Aims of this chapter

Windows 98 gives you a whole host of ways to configure and control the hardware and software on your system. Windows' own installation routine, its 'plug and play' facility for new hardware, and the setup routines that install new software, all help to ensure that your system is properly configured. However, there are some things which Windows cannot do for you as they depend upon your needs and preferences. In the Control Panel you will find two dozen or so components – the actual number depends upon your system – which you can use to customise your setup to suit yourself. In this chapter we will be looking at eight of the key components. Even if you are happy with the way that your system is running – or if you are hesitant about making changes that you might regret – do have a look at these. All the panels have a **Cancel** button!

8.2 Using the Panel

Open the Control Panel by clicking on the **Start** button, pointing to **Settings** and selecting it from there.

Run a component by clicking (or double-clicking) on its icon. This will open the appropriate Properties panel.

View and edit its settings, clicking **OK** at the end to fix the new settings, or **Cancel** to abandon your changes.

Repeat with other components as required – the Control Panel remains open until you close it with **File ➜ Close** or by clicking ▣.

Figure 8.1 The Control Panel. Its contents vary according to the setup of your system – only the common core is covered in this chapter.

8.3 Accessibility

The options here are designed to make life easier for people with disabilities, but are worth investigating by anyone who is less than comfortable with the keyboard or mouse.

Keyboard

StickyKeys allow you to get the **Shift**, **Ctrl** and **Alt** key combinations by pressing them in sequence rather than simultaneously.

FilterKeys control the point at which a keystroke is picked up, or is repeated, and the repeat rate. Most of these settings can also be controlled through the Keyboard component (page103). If you still find that the keys are not responding as you would like after you have set the options there, come back and check out FilterKeys.

ToggleKeys will alert you when the Caps Lock, NumLock or Scroll Lock keys are pressed. This is handy if, like me, you sometimes hit Caps Lock when aiming for Tab, and then type merrily on in CAPITALS!

Set the keyboard options through the **Keyboard Properties** panel before tweaking with **FilterKeys**

The panels that open from the **Settings** buttons vary, of course, but all have a **Keyboard shortcut** option. If used, the feature can be turned on and off – either to suit different users, or to suit the way you are working at that time.

Figure 8.2 The Accessibility options can make your system easier to use, see and hear.

Sound

The main option on this tab turns on visual clues to replace, or emphasise sound prompts.

Display

The high contrast display options, which are also available through the Display Properties panel (Chapter 2), can be turned on here.

Mouse

The MouseKeys option allows you to use the Number pad keys to make mouse actions. The central key (5) does the left click; minus and 5 do the right-click; the number keys (7, 8, 9, 4, 6, 1, 2, 3) move the mouse.

General

If you have set up an accessibility option so that it can be toggled on and off as required, go to this tab to define when to turn options off, and how to notify you of their status. If you have a device plugged into your serial port, to use in place of the standard keyboard or mouse, it can be set up through this tab.

8.4 Add/Remove Programs

Any software that is written to the Windows 95 or 98 specifications will be registered with the system when it is installed, so that it can be uninstalled, or the installation adjusted later through this panel.

Install/Uninstall

New software can be installed through this tab, but can equally well be installed by running the 'install' or 'setup' program directly. It is not normally worth running Add/Remove Programs to do the job.

The main value of Install/Uninstall is in clearing unwanted software off your system, and in adding or removing components from software suites, such as Microsoft Office. If you simply delete a program's folder in Windows Explorer, it may remove all or most of the software's files – though there may be others scattered elsewhere in your disks – but it will not remove the entry in the Start menu, or the File Types associations. A proper uninstall will (normally) do a full clean-out from your system.

Figure 8.3 All properly written Windows 95/98 software can be uninstalled, or its components varied through this tab.

Clicking **Add/Remove** will take you to a routine to select components to add or remove from a suite, or uninstall simpler one-part software

Windows Setup

Windows 98 is a huge package with a vast set of utilities and accessories – most people will use only a limited number of these and no-one will use all of them. If you installed 98 over an earlier version of Windows, you will have made some choices of which components to include. If Windows 98 was installed when you acquired the PC, the selection will have been made for you. Either way, it is quite likely that you will decide, after having used Windows 98 for a while, that some components are a waste of space, but that there are others that you need.

1 Dig out your Windows CD and switch to the **Windows Setup** panel.

2 Select a **Component** heading from the list and click the **Details** button.

3 At the next panel, tick the checkbox to add a component, or clear it to remove an existing one, then click **OK**.

4 Click **OK** on the main panel when you have done, and wait while Windows adds or removes components. You may have to restart the PC for some changes to take effect.

Figure 8.4 Adjusting the Windows setup.

☑ all components selected under this heading

☑ some components selected

☐ no components selected

Outlook Express is a single component – **Details** is greyed out when it is selected

As you select components to add or remove, this keeps a running total of the space freed up or required. The full Windows 98 installation takes over 120Mb. You may have better uses for your disk space.

At this level, hardly any components have a sub-set of options.

8.5 Date/Time

Even if you do not display the Clock on the Taskbar (see page 109), you should still make sure that the clock/calendar is correctly set if you want the date and time details to be right on your saved documents.

PCs are good time-keepers – Windows 98 even adjusts for Summer Time automatically – as long as they are set correctly at the start. Open the Date/Time Properties panel and check yours.

Figure 8.5 Setting the clock and calendar.

To change the time, select the hour, minute or seconds digits and use the arrow buttons.

If the Time Zone is wrong, switch to that tab and select the right one from the list.

8.6 Desktop Themes

These are purely decorative, but can be fun. A theme will give a consistent look to your Desktop, its icons and screen saver, as well as mouse pointers, sounds and the fonts used in Windows – though you don't have to apply all aspects of the theme. Themes are installed onto the disk through the Windows Setup routine. This lets you select which one to use.

1 Select the theme from the drop-down list at the top.
2 Preview the screen saver, mouse pointers and sounds.
3 Clear the checkboxes for any parts that you do not want.
4 Click **Apply** if you want to see the theme in place before finally committing yourself – if you don't like it, start again.
5 Click **OK**.

Figure 8.6 If you use all aspects of a theme, your Desktop will have a more consistent appearance but may not be as clear as you might like! It is just as well that the icons here are labelled.

8.7 Fonts

A font is a typeface design, identified by a name. Within one font you will get type in a range of sizes (some are more variable than others), and the appearance may be varied by the use of bold, italic or other styles.

Fonts can be divided into three categories:

- **Serif** – like this (Times New Roman), marked by little tails at the ends of strokes. The tails (serifs) make the text easier to read, which is why serif fonts are normally chosen for large blocks of text.

- **Sans serif** – like this (Arial), with simpler lines. Sans fonts are typically used for headings and captions.

- **Display** – *decorative* fonts of all kinds. These are mainly used for headlines, posters, adverts, party invitations and special effects.

There are thousands of fonts in the world, and a couple of dozen of the best of these are supplied with Windows 98. You will get more with any word processing and page layout software that you install, and you can buy CDs full of fonts.

In practice, you do not need a huge number. Professional designers normally work to the 'three-font' rule: no more than three fonts on any one page – one serif, one sans serif and one display – using different sizes and styles for variety and emphasis. It may well be a different set of three fonts for each project, but three or four serif and sans fonts and a dozen or so display fonts should be enough for most purposes. The more you have, the longer it will take to scroll through the font list whenever you are formatting text!

Do include Times New Roman and **Arial** in your selection. These two are used far more often than any others, simply because they are clear, attractive and highly readable. They are also – along with `Courier New` – the standard fonts for Web pages.

Some fonts have Bold, Italic and Bold Italic variations. Within a word-processor you will normally only see the main name in the font list – the Bold or Italic versions are then used if these effects are selected later.

Figure 8.7 The Fonts folder, here using the *List by similarity* view. Choose a font from the drop-down list, and the whole set is then listed in order of closeness of match. This view is useful for weeding out excess fonts – to remove an unwanted font, select it then use **Delete** on the **File** menu.

Viewing fonts

If you want to see what a font looks like, just click on it. A viewer will open, showing samples of the characters in a range of sizes. If the font is to be used for extensive work, and it is especially important that it looks just right, click the **Print** button to get a printed copy – there are often subtle differences between the screen display and printed output.

Figure 8.8 The font viewer in use. True Type fonts are virtually identical on screen and paper. If they are not True Type, they are more likely to vary. In any case, a test print is often worth having.

Click **Done** or to close the viewer, or select another font – a second copy of the viewer will open – if you want to compare them side by side.

Installing fonts

If you have bought fonts on disk or CD-ROM, or have downloaded them from the Internet, they must be installed properly before they can be used.

1 Open the **File** menu and select **Install New Font**.

2 At the **Add Fonts** panel, select the drive and folder.

3 Select the fonts from the list, holding down **Ctrl** while you click if you want to pick several.

Click **Select All** if there are only a few – and you want them all.

If there are Bold and Italic variations, select them as well as the main font.

4 If the font file is already on your hard disk, clear the **Copy fonts to Fonts folder** checkbox. There is no point in duplicating storage.

5 Click **OK**.

8.8 Keyboard

How long your fingers linger on the keys affects the way that keystrokes are repeated. You will want most keystrokes to be picked up separately, but sometimes you want them to repeat – perhaps to create a dividing line of *******. Use this panel to set the keyboard response to suit your fingers.

■ The **Repeat delay** is how long to wait before starting to repeat – if you are heavy-fingered, set this to *Long*.

■ The **Repeat rate** is how fast the characters are produced. This should match your reaction times.

Test the settings by typing in the test area, before you click **OK**.

8.9 Mouse

Buttons

The only crucial setting here is the **Double-click** speed. Test the current setting by double-clicking on the jack-in-the-box, and use the slider to adjust the response if necessary.

Figure 8.9 Use the **Keyboard** panel to set the response speed to suit you.

If you sometimes write in a different language, use the **Language** tab to set up the keyboard to toggle between two character sets.

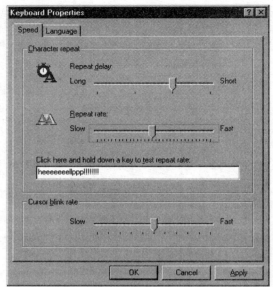

Figure 8.10 The **Buttons** tab of the **Mouse** panel. When the double-click speed is set correctly, you should be able to get the jack in and out of the box effortlessly.

You can switch the buttons over if you are left-handed, but it is better to get used to the standard layout, unless you only ever use the one PC. (Switching to the left-handed layout will also thoroughly confuse anyone else who tries to use the machine!)

Pointers

The options here are almost entirely decorative, though obviously anything which makes is easier for you to see what you are doing must be beneficial. There are a dozen or so pointers, each related to a different mouse action. If you do not like some or all of the current set, select them one at a time and click **Browse**. You can then pick a new one from the pointers folder.

Preview pane – use it to view animated cursors.

If you don't like a pointer, select it and browse for an alternative.

Motion

The **Pointer speed** pane controls how far and how fast the pointer moves in relation to the mouse movement. To test this out, move the mouse and watch the pointer. If you don't feel comfortably in control of it, drag the slider towards Slow. If it's taking too long to get around the screen, set it faster. Click **Apply** and test again. Click **OK** when it feels right.

The **Pointer trail** option is only really relevant for laptop users. Pointers do not show up well on LCD screens, particularly when they are in motion. Turning on the trail makes them much easier to see.

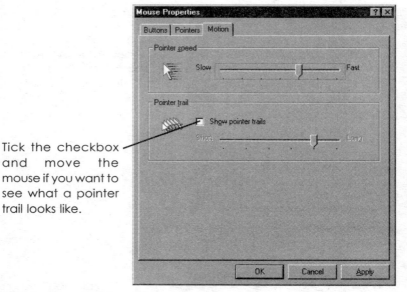

Tick the checkbox and move the mouse if you want to see what a pointer trail looks like.

8.10 Sounds

Windows can attach sounds to certain events so that you get, for example, a fanfare at start up and a warning noise when you are about to do something you may later regret. Some of these are just for fun, others can be very useful. If you tend to watch the keyboard, rather than the screen, when you are typing, then an audible warning will alert you to a situation before it becomes a problem.

The Sounds Properties panel is where you decide which events are to be accompanied by a sound, and which sounds to use.

Figure 8.11 Selecting a new sound to attach to an event. If you do not want any sound, select *None* in the **Name** textbox of the Sounds panel.

8.11 Summary

- You can configure your system to suit your way of working through the components of the Control Panel.
- The Accessibility options can make the keyboard easier to use and the screen easier to see.
- Use the Add/Remove Programs panel to uninstall unwanted software and to add or remove the components of application suites and of Windows.
- If you PC displays the wrong date or time, adjust it through the Date/Time panel.
- The Desktop Themes are mainly for fun – and why not?
- The Fonts icon opens the Fonts folder where you can view fonts, remove unwanted ones and install new ones.
- Test and adjust the response rate of the keyboard through the Keyboard panel.
- Use the Mouse panel to set the double-click response and the speed at which the mouse moves the pointer. New pointer icons can be selected here.
- Sounds can be attached to events to alert you when things happen.

OTHER CONTROL PANEL COMPONENTS

Other key components have been or will be dealt with in other chapters, where they are directly related to the aspect of Windows being covered. For **Display**, see Chapter 2; **Internet** and **Modems**, Chapter 10; **Printers**, Chapter 13.

The **System** properties, though crucial to the correct running of your PC, are best left to Windows – look, but don't touch!

9 | TASKBAR AND START MENU SETTINGS

9.1 Aims of this chapter

By now you should be familiar with using the Taskbar and Start menu in your Windows sessions. In this chapter we will look at ways in which you can customise the Taskbar and reorganise the Start menu. The techniques are simple and worth learning – these are two elements of the Windows system that you will use regularly, so you should have them set up to your way of working.

9.2 Taskbar options

The Properties panel for the Taskbar and Start menu can be opened either from the **Start → Settings** submenu, or by right-clicking the Taskbar and selecting **Properties**.

The Taskbar tab has only four on/off options, and you can see their effects, as you set them, in the preview pane.

- **Always on top** – if set, the Taskbar overlaps any windows that reach the bottom of the screen.
- **Auto hide** – if set, the Taskbar slides off-screen when not in use. Pointing off the screen makes it pop-up again when wanted.
- **Show small icons in Start menu** – turn this off for more visible icons.
- **Show clock** – displays the clock in the far right of the Taskbar. Note that it you point to the clock, the date will pop up.

Figure 9.1 Setting the Taskbar options. If you have a small screen, either turn off **Always on top** or turn on **Auto hide** to maximise your working area.

9.3 Toolbars

In its initial settings, the Taskbar will have one toolbar on it – **Quick Launch** (see page 5). More can be added if you want to be able to start more applications from the Taskbar. There are four ready-made toolbars.

- **Address** – enter an Internet address here, and Internet Explorer will start and try to connect to it.
- **Links** – carries a set of buttons with Internet addresses, clicking one starts Internet Explorer to make the connection.
- **Desktop** – contains copies of the icons present on the Desktop.
- **Quick Launch** – for starting the main Internet applications.

Right-click on any blank area of the Taskbar to open the short menu

Figure 9.2 The Taskbar with the Links and Desktop toolbars added. Click the arrowheads on the right to scroll the bars.

Toolbar options

The short menu that can be opened from a toolbar contains the usual Taskbar items, plus a small set of options that control the appearance of the toolbar.

View – **Large** or **Small** sets the icon size.

Show Text – adds labels.

Refresh – simply redraws the toolbar.

Open – opens the toolbar's folder so that you can add or remove shortcuts.

Show Title – displays the toolbar's title.

Creating new toolbars

If you like working from the Taskbar, you can set up one or more toolbars containing shortcuts to your favourite applications, folders – or Internet links (see Chapter 10):

1 Create a folder, named 'My Programs' or something similar.
2 Setup shortcuts to the chosen applications or folders – hold the right button down as you drag the icons into this folder, and select the **Create Shortcut Here** option.

Program files are sometimes hard to find – if they are not in the main folder, look for a 'Bin'. Binary (program) files are often kept in one.

Figure 9.3 Creating a shortcut for the new toolbar.

Figure 9.4 The new toolbar folder, ready to be added to the Taskbar.

3 If you are going to show Text labels on the toolbar, edit the
   names so that they are as brief as possible or you will have
   trouble displaying them all.

4 When you have assembled
   your shortcuts, right-click
   on the **Taskbar**, point to
   Toolbars and select **New
   Toolbar...**

5 Work through the folder display to find the one containing
   your shortcuts.

6 Click **OK**.

Figure 9.5 Adding the new
toolbar. You could create
several toolbars, one for each
of the PC's users, or to suit the
different kinds of work that
you do on the machine.

9.4 Moving and resizing

The Taskbar is normally a thin bar across the bottom of the screen, and this works very well when it is used only for the Quick Launch toolbar and a few application buttons. Add more toolbars and it is going to get crowded and difficult to use. There are two possible solutions:

■ Make the Taskbar deeper by dragging its top edge upwards. The toolbars can be rearranged within this area by dragging on their handles. Move them up or down between the lines, or drag sideways to adjust their relative sizes.

Drag the edge to change the depth

Drag on a handle to move a toolbar
or to make it wider/narrower

■ Move the Taskbar to one or other side of the screen. By default it will be wide enough to show the Text labels on the icons. You will probably need to adjust the layout by dragging on the handles between the sections, and may want to make the bar slimmer – drag its edge inwards.

DO YOU NEED LABELS?

If the icons are clear enough, the toolbar titles and shortcut labels are not really necessary. Turning them off will save a lot of space, allowing you to pack more into a slim Taskbar.

9.5 The Start menu

If you open the Taskbar Properties panel and switch to the **Start Menu Programs** tab, you can control which items appear on your Start menu system, and where they appear.

Figure 9.6 The Start Menu Programs tab. The main routines are reached through the buttons in the Customize area.

Click the **Clear** button in the Documents area whenever you want to wipe the slate clean.

Adding

This is the fiddliest of these three jobs, but fortunately not one that you will have to do very often – with modern software, the installation routines normally add the Start menu entries for you.

- Before you start, locate the application's main file, using Explorer or My Computer. It will be easier to find it through one of these than at the Browse dialog in step 2.
1 Click **Add**. This starts a wizard to guide you through the process.
2 At the **Create Shortcut** stage, click **Browse** and locate the program file. Click **OK**, then click **Next** at the wizard panel.
3 Select the Start menu folder – opening them as necessary to reach subfolders (submenus) – and click **Next**.
4 Finally, type a name for the menu item and click **Finish**.

If you know the folder and file-name, you can type it in, but browsing is usually simpler and more accurate.

In this case, I could have typed in **C:\Program Files\Iview\Lviewp1b.exe** instead of browsing for it.

The menus are presented as folders – open them as needed to reach the right place.

Figure 9.7 The main stages of the Add routine. If you make a mistake at any point, click **Back** to redo a stage.

Removing

Start menus can get cluttered and messy. Some installation routines don't just put in entries for the applications, they also create shortcuts to the 'Readme' file (that you will read once, if at all) and to the Help pages (that you normally only open from within the application). Some uninstall routines fail to remove the entries from the Start menu when the program files are deleted. Some software creates duplicate entries in the main menu and in submenus.

Removing entries is very simple.

1 At the Start Menu Programs tab, click **Remove**.

2 Open up the folders to display the unwanted entries.

3 Select a folder or menu item and click **Remove**.

4 Repeat as necessary.

5 Click **Close**.

Reorganising the menus

The Start menu system is stored as a set of folders and subfolders in the *C:\Windows\Start Menu* folder. You can open it in Explorer or My Computer, though it is probably simpler to click the **Advanced** button on the **Start Menu Programs** tab. This opens a limited version of Explorer. You cannot move up out of the Start Menu folder, but all the normal file management techniques for moving, deleting and renaming files and folders work here.

If you have installed so many applications that your Start menu has become overcrowded, create 'group' folders and move the entries and folders of related applications into these. A short main menu that leads to two or three levels of submenus is much easier to work with than one huge menu!

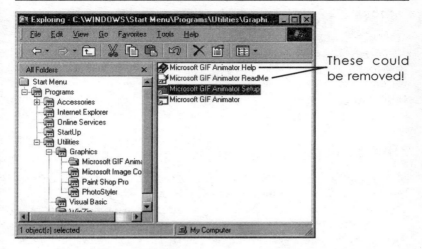

These could be removed!

Figure 9.8 The **Advanced** button lets you explore the Start menu. In the example, the graphics packages' folders have all been moved into a Graphics folder, which is one of several in the Utilities folder.

9.6 Summary

- Taskbar can be displayed on top of all other windows, behind them, or tucked off screen when not in use.
- Ready-made toolbars can be added to the Taskbar.
- You can create your own folders of shortcuts and turn them into Taskbar toolbars.
- You can adjust the depth and position of the Taskbar, and move the toolbars within it.
- Entries can be added to or removed from the Start menu.
- The menu structure can be reorganised using the normal file management techniques.

10 INTERNET EXPLORER

10.1 Aims of this chapter

This chapter concentrates on the practical aspects of getting online through Windows 98, and on setting up and using Internet Explorer. We will have a brief look at some of the facilities that can be reached through the Internet, but there isn't room in this book to tackle this huge area properly. If you want to know more about the Internet, try *Teach Yourself The Internet*.

10.2 What is the Internet?

The Internet is a world-wide communications network, linking thousands of computer networks, through a mixture of private and public phone lines and microwave links. Its component networks are run by government agencies, universities and commercial organisations, working co-operatively and loosely controlled by the Internet Society. These organisations bring many millions of people onto the Internet, and millions more link in their home computers through one or other of the many service providers.

At the time of writing, mid-1998, there are over 16 million host computers supplying services and information over the Net, and the number of users is estimated to be upwards of 50 million. In the UK alone, there are over 200,000 host computers on the Internet, and around 4 million people have access either from home, or through their work or through their school or university.

The Internet can be accessed and used in a number of ways. For most people, the most important aspects of the Internet are the World Wide Web, electronic mail and newsgroups. Once you get into it, you will soon discover that there are other ways to use the Internet and you might want to investigate some of these over time.

The World Wide Web

This is probably the most exciting and useful aspect of the Internet for most users. It consists of hundred of millions of *pages* of information, stored on host computers throughout the world. The pages contain text, graphics, video clips, sounds and – most importantly – *hyperlinks* to other pages. Clicking on a hyperlink will take you to another page, which may be in the same computer, or in one a thousand miles away.

Some Web pages are excellent sources of information in their own right, some are treasure troves of links to other valuable pages; and some are pure trivia. You have to be selective, and you have to keep an eye on the phone bill, for Web browsing is a fascinating, but time-consuming activity.

To access the Web you need a browser – such as Internet Explorer – which can display the text and images, and interpret the links that will take you from one page to another.

Finding stuff

Despite the massive quantity of information that is available on the Web, finding the things that interest you is not usually that difficult. There are several *directories*, which hold large sets of organised links to Web pages – and to other parts of the Internet. Yahoo (page 135) is probably the best known of these, and is an excellent place at which to start researching a subject. There are also *search engines* where you can hunt for pages that contain given words. They are most useful when you are looking for information on a very specific topic as they can pick out the relevant pages from the millions on the Web. Internet Explorer has links to some of the best search engines (see page 134).

On-line sales and services

The World Wide Web is becoming a good place to do business. New companies have been started to sell goods over the Web (books, CDs, fancy gifts, and computer hardware and software seem to do best at present) and an increasing number of existing shops and other firms are now marketing their goods and services online. Fraud is a problem on the Internet, but probably no more so than it is in any area where business is done. You can shop and deal as safely over the Internet as you can by mail order or in the high street. It's largely a matter of choosing your firms wisely and avoiding too-good-to-be-true bargains.

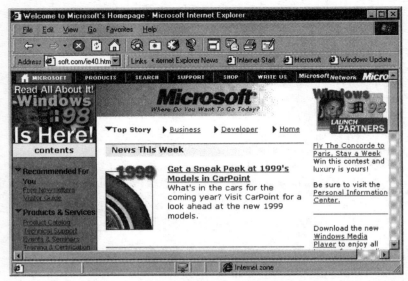

Figure 10.1 Microsoft runs an extensive Web site – a great source of information and software, with links to many resources beyond its site.

Your own Home Page

Almost all Internet service providers offer their subscribers the opportunity to have their own home pages. Some people use the pages as notice boards for their local sports or hobby clubs; some run fan clubs on theirs; some will pull together information and links on a subject, making their home pages into valuable resources for others who share their interests.

If you want to create your own home page, you will need some understanding of *HTML* (HyperText Markup Language) – the coding system behind Web pages. It is not difficult to learn, and you don't need to learn much if you use FrontPage Express, or other HTML editor. This will handle the nitty gritty of the HTML system and let you get on with the job of designing the layout and producing the content.

E-mail

Electronic mail is probably the most widely used of all the Internet facilities – after the novelty of browsing the Web has worn thin, you will still be logging on regularly to collect and send e-mail! E-mail is mainly used for sending plain text messages, but you can also send formatted text, and attach graphics, sounds and other data files to your messages.

Most e-mail is one-to-one communication, but there are also mail lists that circulate messages to their members. Each of the many hundreds of lists covers a specialist interest, and almost all are open to anyone to join.

Newsgroups

These are a development of mail lists, and have much in common with them. There are thousands of newsgroups (over 20,000 at the last count), covering an amazing range of interests, activities and obsessions, from the mundane to the bizarre. Some newsgroups are very active, with hundreds of new articles every day; others have much lighter traffic. Some groups clearly have members with too much free time and free access to the Internet; in others, the articles are typically brief but relevant and interesting. Some groups are moderated – i.e. they have someone to edit submissions and filter out the irrelevant ones. Unmoderated groups on topics that attract obsessives can produce vast quantities of articles that are of little interest to anyone but their authors.

You may not have access to all the Internet's newsgroups. You can only reach those that are handled by the news server at your service provider, and some providers are more selective than others. Some may even offer you the option of accessing only those that are suitable for family audiences – an option worth considering if children use your Internet connection.

10.3 Getting online

Windows 98 has all the software that you need to access the Internet. To actually get online from home, you will also need:

- a modem – to convert computer signals into a form that can be sent down the phone lines. If your PC is not already equipped with one, a modem is easily added. Expect to pay around £150 for a fast (56K) modem, or half as much for a 28.8K modem. (The Internet's connections are often so busy that faster modems rarely get the chance to run at full speed!)
- a phone socket within reach of your computer.

■ an account with an Internet service provider. This gives you access to the Internet and an e-mail address. It will cost you around £15 a month for unlimited time online, or £6–£7 for limited hours, with excess time charged by the minute.

Online services

If you open the **Online Services** folder on the Desktop, you will find shortcuts to four service providers, and a shortcut to a fifth, Microsoft Network, should be directly on your Desktop. Selecting any of these will install their special software, and let you sign up to the service. The process is almost completely automated – basically all you will need to do is give your own details.

CompuServe and AOL (America Online) both offer a free month's trial to prospective members. You will have to give your credit card number when you sign up, but if you decide that the service does not suit you, or you would like to try some others first, the subscription can be cancelled before the trial period is up.

MSN (MicroSoft Network) may seem to be an obvious choice for Windows users, but its future is in some doubt. At the time of writing, Microsoft is apparently considering pulling out of access provision. If they do, existing members will be transferred to another service provider, while MSN will continue just as a content provider – their site will still be offering news, views, software and other services.

These are by no means the only Internet service providers. If you look in any PC or Internet magazine you will find plenty of others, some of which also offer free trial membership. Those that offer members-only online services, may supply special software. With others, you simply use the standard Windows 98 software – Internet Explorer and Outlook Express. Some providers may supply you with an installation disk, to set up the connection, but don't worry if you have to do it yourself – it's easy.

THINK LOCAL

If you have a local service provider, give them a ring and see what they have to offer. A small local service may well give a better level of support and assistance than a national firm.

Figure 10.2 CompuServe offers a wide range of services to its members, and has special software to handle these. You can also reach the wider Internet through Compuserve.

10.4 Setting up a Connection

Internet Connection Wizard

This can be used to find a service provider or to set up a connection to an existing provider. As with all wizards, work through it stage by stage, supplying information or making choices in response to prompts.

- If you are in doubt about anything, accept the default settings.
- Don't touch the **Advanced Settings** unless the provider tells you exactly what to do! Most should work with the defaults.
- If you think you have made a mistake at any stage, click the **Back** button to check and correct earlier entries – or if it's a really crucial mistake, click **Cancel** and start again!
- If you are going to use this to find a provider, you will need persistence and patience. It can take many attempts before

you get through to Microsoft's online referral service, where
the list of providers is kept!

■ If you have already set up an account with a provider, make
  sure that you have at hand any information they sent to you –
  including their phone number, mail and news servers' names,
  your user details. This is normally all that's needed, but some
  providers may give you technical details. Have them ready.

■ You will be offered the chance to set up your mail, news and
  Internet directory service. Mail and news are worth doing.
  The directory service could well be left until later.

To run the Wizard, click **Start**, point to **Programs**, then **Internet Explorer**
and select **Connection Wizard**.

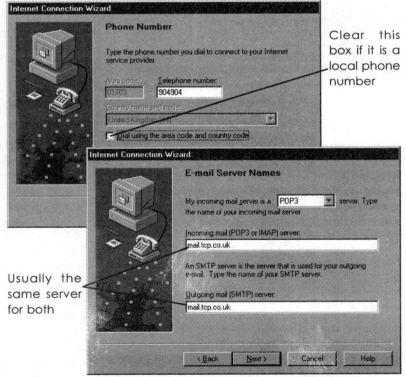

Figure 10.3 Two stages (of many) from the Connection Wizard.

TROUBLE CONNECTING?

If you have any difficulties in establishing a working connection
with your provider, look for the Modem Troubleshooter in the
Help pages. It will show you what to check, and what to try to
solve the problem. If that fails, ring your provider's technical
support line – patience is a virtue with most of these.

10.5 Internet Explorer

You can access the Internet from many places in the Windows 98 system,
but the main tool for this job is Internet Explorer. It is very similar to
Windows Explorer or My Computer – especially when using Web page
view. In fact, if you use the Favorites, Links buttons or Address box to
connect to an Internet site through either Windows Explorer or My
Computer, they will effectively turn into Internet Explorer.

■ Microsoft would like you to view the Internet as an extension
   of your Desktop. If you connect through an ISDN line, or
   better still a fast, high-capacity leased line that is permanently
   open, then this may be a viable view. If you connect by
   dialling in to a service provider, the transition from Desktop
   to Internet will rarely be smooth.

For the rest of this chapter, I'll concentrate on Internet Explorer, but it's
worth bearing in mind that this is not the only route into the Net.

Internet Explorer is designed for fast, easy navigation, both on and offline.
When you browse a page, its files are stored in a temporary folder on your
hard disk. When you return to the same page, its files are then loaded from
the disk, rather than downloaded from the Internet. This makes browsing
far, far quicker! We all have our own favourite places that we use to start
searching for stuff, and when following up links you will often find pages
with several good leads, and you will want to return to these to pick up
new trails. These stored files also allow you to 'revisit' sites when you are
offline, but it should be noted that this does not always work. Some pages
insist on downloading new files – typically adverts – each time they are
opened, and will not display without them.

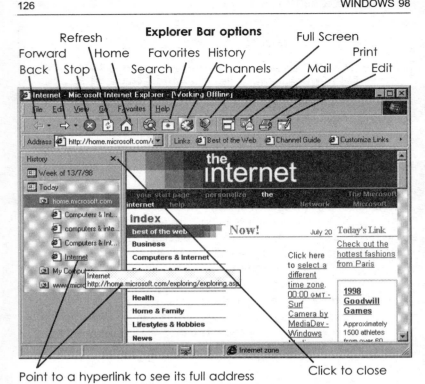

Point to a hyperlink to see its full address   Click to close

Figure 10.4 The Internet Explorer display. The Explorer bar panel on the left can be opened to display the History list (pages visited recently), Favorites, an online Search facility or Channels (sites which send pages to you, rather than you having to go to them).

The Internet Explorer window

- The **Standard**, **Address** and **Links toolbars** can be turned on or off – the Address (page 137) is more useful here than it is in Windows Explorer.

- The **Explorer Bar** can display Search (page 134), Favorites (page 138), History (page 138) or Channels (page 139).

- For maximum viewing area when browsing, switching to **Full Screen View** will turn off all the features of the window, except the Standard toolbar.

The Standard toolbar

These buttons contain almost all of the controls that you need when you are online.

- **Back** and **Forward** move between the pages already visited during the session.
- **Stop** – use it when you realise at the start of a long download that you don't really want to see that page.
- **Refresh** redraws the current page.
- **Home** goes to your start page – your jumping off point into the Web. This can be your own home page or any other.
- The **Explorer bar** buttons open the bar to run a Search, browse the Favorites or History Folder, or use the Channels.
- **Full Screen** toggles between Full Screen and normal view.
- **Mail** starts or switches to your mail software (normally Outlook Express).
- **Print** prints the current page (text and graphics).
- **Edit** can only be used with pages which have been saved as a file on disk – and normally they will be ones you have written. Edit takes the page into FrontPage Express (if installed) or other editor/word processor.

Menu commands

Most of the ones that you will use regularly are duplicated by the Toolbar buttons, and are better handled through them. However, there are some very useful commands that can only be reached through the menus:

- **File → New → Window** opens a second browser window, so that you can keep one page at hand while you follow up other leads.
- **File → Work Offline** should be turned on when using Explorer offline.
- **Edit → Find** will search for words in the current page.
- **View → Fonts** lets you set the size of the text (headlines are scaled to match); foreign alphabets can be turned on here.

File → Open, View → Internet Options and the **Favorites** commands are also important. We will return to them in the next few pages.

10.6 Internet Options

These options can be set or changed at any time on or offline (though the odd couple only take effect after you restart the PC). A few should be set before you start to use Explorer in earnest, others are best left until you have been using it for a while and have a clearer idea of what settings best suit your preferred way of working.

- Use **View → Internet Options** to open the panel, and click on the tab names to move between the sets of options.

- If you set options that change the appearance of the screen, click **Apply** to see how they look.

- Only click **OK** when you have finished with all the tabs.

General

The **Home page** defines where Explorer goes when it is first started. This could be a personalised start page at Microsoft (or other content provider – many offer this facility), your own home page, or a blank page if each session is a new voyage. An address can be typed in here, but it is simpler to wait until you are online at the right place, then just come back to this tab and click **Use Current**.

In **Temporary Internet files**, click **Settings** to define how Explorer handles page files.

- In the **Check for newer version of stored pages**, select *Every visit to the page*, if the pages you use a lot change frequently.

- The **Amount of disk space to use** depends upon how much browsing you do, how often you return to pages and how much space you have. When the space is used up, older files are wiped to make way for new ones. A typical page of text and graphics might add up to 50Kb – say 20 pages per Mb. How many pages do you want in store – remembering that, if you update pages when you revisit, those that you use regularly will be relatively new files.

- If you have more spare space on a second hard disk, click Move Folder and set up the temporary storage space there.

The History records your movements, to allow easier revisiting – how long do you want to keep it?

Set the Colors, Fonts and Accessibility options if you need a high visibility display.

If you tend to visit pages that have a lot of graphics or information, and you want to be able to study these later, offline, set a high disk space level.

Figure 10.5 Setting the **General** options.

Security

The Internet is basically a safe place – as long as you take a few sensible precautions. If you spend most of your time at major commercial and other well-established sites, and at ones they recommend, security should not be a major concern. If you browse more widely, you may bump up against the mischievous and the unscrupulous. The main dangers are these:

- **Viruses** – You can only get these from executable files (programs) or macros, and only when you run them. You cannot pick up a virus simply by browsing a page or reading e-mail or news articles. A virus-checker will give you an extra level of protection.
- **Active content** – Web designers may use small programs (applets), written in Java, Javascript or ActiveX to enhance their pages – though many are just decorative. The languages are designed to be secure – the programs should not be able to access your system – but hackers do find loopholes.
- **Privacy intrusions** – Every time you fill in a form online, run a search or make a choice, you send some information about yourself along with the intended data. Some sites may attempt to store and misuse this information.
- **Cookies** – A cookie is a short file, written by a site onto your hard disk. They are normally used to store your personal preferences at that site – so that when you revisit you don't have to set preferences again – or simply to log your visit. You don't have to accept cookies (see page 134).

Zones and security levels

If you have a **local intranet** (Web site within the organisation and only open to its members), this zone can be set to *Low* security.

The **Internet zone** cover all unclassified sites (initially everywhere) and should be set to *High* or *Medium* security.

Sites that you know and trust can be added to the **Trusted sites zone**, and its level set to *Low*.

If your Internet zone setting is at Medium, any sites that you are wary of – but still want to revisit – should be added to the **restricted sites zones**, and its level set to *High*.

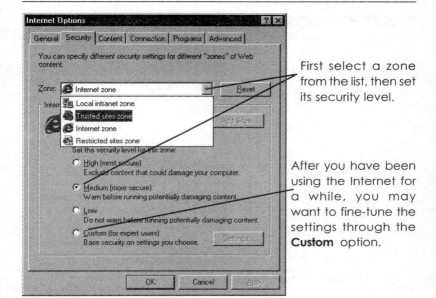

First select a zone from the list, then set its security level.

After you have been using the Internet for a while, you may want to fine-tune the settings through the **Custom** option.

Figure 10.6 The **Security** tab – when in doubt, play safe!

Content Advisor and safe surfing

If children can get online from your PC, you may want to enable the Content Advisor to set limits to the types of material that they can access through the Internet.

The Content Advisor allows you to restrict unsupervised access to those sites which have been rated by the Recreational Software Advisory Council for the Internet (RASCi). This rates sites an a scale of 1 to 5 for language, nudity, sex and violence. You set the limits of what may be accessed from your machine.

Many perfectly acceptable sites do not have a rating, simply because they have not applied for one, but this is not a major problem. It just means that the kids will have to ask someone who knows the password to override the restrictions when they find somewhere good but unrated. And if you want to browse unrestricted, you can disable the advisor.

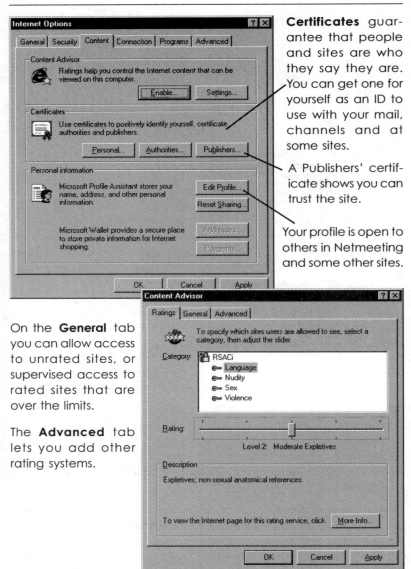

Certificates guarantee that people and sites are who they say they are. You can get one for yourself as an ID to use with your mail, channels and at some sites.

A Publishers' certificate shows you can trust the site.

Your profile is open to others in Netmeeting and some other sites.

On the **General** tab you can allow access to unrated sites, or supervised access to rated sites that are over the limits.

The **Advanced** tab lets you add other rating systems.

Figure 10.7 The **Content** tab. Turn on **Content Advisor** if you are going to let children have unsupervised access to the Internet.

SAFER SURFING

If you are concerned about people reaching the murkier corners of the Internet, Content Advisor is only the first line of defence. For more about child safety, browse over to http://www.safekids.com.

Advanced

Most of the **Advanced** options should be left well alone until you really know what you are doing, but there are a couple that you might want to look at now.

In the **Multimedia** section, turn off the **Play** options for faster browsing. Turning **Show Pictures** off will also improve downloading times, but pictures often carry essential information and hyperlinks. With **Show Pictures** off, you can download an individual picture by clicking on the ▓ which appears in its place.

Figure 10.8 Most **Advanced** options should be left at their defaults – click **Restore Defaults** if you think you may have messed them up!

If you don't want to accept **Cookies,** you can disable them. Should you find that there are some sites that you can only use properly if you accept cookies – there are plenty of clubs and user groups that use them as IDs – then switch to '**Prompt before accepting**'. It will slow things down but leave you in control.

In the **Java** section, the **Java JIT compiler** should be enabled if you want to run any Java applets that you meet.

10.7 Browsing the Web

Starting from Microsoft

Hypertext links provide an efficient means of following threads from page to page, but with so much information spread over so many pages on so many sites over the Web, the problem is where to start looking. Internet Explorer has ready-made links to some good start points at the Microsoft site, including their **Web directory**, with sets of links organised by topics – the **Best of the Web** button will take you there. Select a topic from the 'best of the web' list, then pick a category. At the next level you will find a set of links that will take you out of Microsoft into the wider Web.

The directory approach is good for starting research on general topics, but if you are looking for specific material, you are probably better off running a search. Internet Explorer offers a simple way to search at five of the leading search engines and directories.

Infoseek	excellent for text-based information.
Lycos	has indexed over 90% of the Web!
UKplus	for UK firms and organisations.
Yell	centred on Electronic Yellow Pages.
Yahoo	the original and the best.

Running a search

1 Click the � button to start the Search in the Explorer bar.
2 Type a word or phrase to describe what you are looking for.
3 Select a place to search.
4 Click the **Search** button.
5 When you get the results, click on a link to view the page in the main window.

Figure 10.9 The main panel shows one of the index pages at **Microsoft's Web directory**. As this didn't yield anything on Koi carp, I've started to run a search at Yahoo, from the Explorer bar.

Other start points

Microsoft's Best of the Web and Search facilities are not the only places to start browsing the Internet. There are others that are well worth a visit.

> Go direct to Yahoo UK & Ireland, at
> **http://www.yahoo.com**
> For child-safe, 'Green Light' sites, try Magellan at
> **http://www.mckinley.com**
> The leading directory in the UK is UKDirectory, at
> **http://www.ukdirectory.co.uk**
> The most comprehensive search engine is AltaVista at
> **http://altavista.digital.com**
> Try Netscape for software, as well as a good starting links, at
> **http://www.netscape.com**

But before you can get to these, you need to know about URLs. Read on!

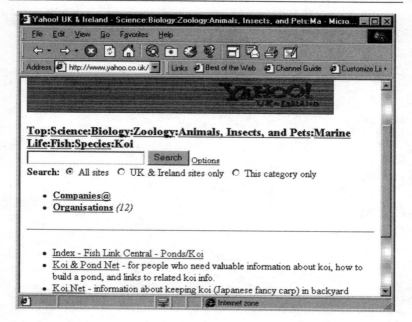

Figure 10.10 Yahoo is one of the best directories and by far the most popular – Yahoo averages around 70 million page views every day!

Uniform Resource Locators (URL)

With all the millions of Web pages, files and other resources that can be reached over the Internet, a standardised way of identifying them is essential. URLs provide this. There are different styles of URL for each approach to the Internet, though they all follow much the same pattern:

```
type://hostcomputer/directory/filename
```

Web pages

Many of these are instantly recognisable from their *html* or *htm* endings, which shows that they are hypertext pages.

```
http://sunsite.unc.edu/boutell/faq/www-faq.html
```

This one is a list of frequently asked questions (*faq*) and their answers, about the World Wide Web (*www*), stored in the Sun archives in the University of North Carolina (*unc*).

The URL of the top page of a site may just consist of the site address, with an (optional) slash at the end. This is the opening page at Microsoft's site:

http://www.microsoft.com/

If you know the URL of a page, you can jump directly to it.

Use **File→ Open**, and type the URL into the panel, or type it into the **Address** toolbar.

The leading http:// is not really necessary. The browser expects you to enter a World Wide Web URL. Thus the URL:

http://www.yahoo.com

can be entered as:

www.yahoo.com

URLs must be typed exactly right for the routine to work. They are not case-sensitive – WWW.YAHOO.COM works just as well as www.yahoo.com – but watch out for symbols. Some URLs include a tilde (~). Where the URL is for the top page of a site, it will end with a slash (/). This can be omitted.

Finding URLs

Before you can use a URL, you have to know it. There are several possible sources:

- As you browse the Web, you may find a hyperlink to a page that you do not want to visit at the time, but might like to drop in on later. Point to it, to display its URL in the Status bar, and make a note of it.

- If you join any **newsgroups** (Chapter 11), you will often see postings about relevant pages on the newsgroup area of interest, particularly new ones.

- Internet magazines and newspaper columns often have 'What's new' features.

History

When you want to return to a page, the simplest way is through the Back button and the list that drops down from it. This only works with those visited very recently – the Back list is wiped at the end of a session, and can be corrupted by movements within sites, especially those with complex, interactive page layouts. The most reliable way to revisit pages is by opening the History list in the Explorer Bar. The pages are grouped by day and then by site, making it easy to find the one you want.

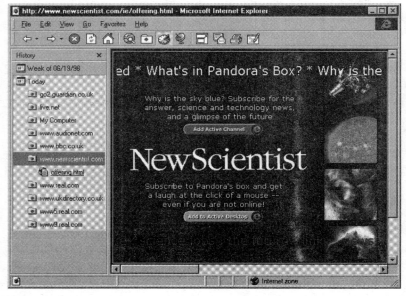

Figure 10.11 Using the **History** list. IE 4.0 groups the pages into their sites, making it much easier to find them.

Favorites

The Explorer Bar can also be used to display the Favorites list. This has a few sets of ready-made links, but is really intended as a store of links to those places that you like to revisit regularly.

- When you find a page that you know you will want again in future, open the **Favorites** menu and select **Add to Favorites**.

- Click **OK** at the **Add Favorite** panel to add the page to the end of the Favorites menu.
- Click **Create in>>** to open the full panel, where you can choose in which folder to store the link – a new folder can be created, if needed.

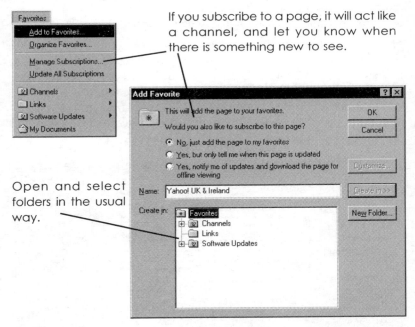

If you subscribe to a page, it will act like a channel, and let you know when there is something new to see.

Open and select folders in the usual way.

Figure 10.12 Adding a page to the **Favorites**. If – more likely when – your Favorites folders get crowded and messy, use **Organise Favorites** to open a Windows Explorer display of the folders. You can then move, rename, delete and generally sort out your stored links.

Channels

The last and, for most people, the least important use of the Explorer Bar is for channels. A channel is a site which sends out new and updated pages to its subscribers, on a regular basis. In theory, this should be easier than having to go to sites to get the information for yourself. The channel files are downloaded in the background, organised and stored, and can then be read at leisure on or offline.

In practice, it only really works in organisations with a fast, permanent connection to the Internet. The channels can then be set to update automatically, at a time when the PC will be idle or at least not being used intensively. If you connect through a dial-up line, subscription is not normally an efficient use of phone time as you tend to get far more information than you want. Downloading channels will also slow down any other browsing if you are trying to do it at the same time.

You may have guessed, I'm not a channel fan, but not many people are. It's worth noting that Netscape, the other big browser producer, has dropped its channel facility from the latest version of its browser. But don't take my word for it, try a channel or two yourself. To subscribe, go online, open the Channels in the Explorer Bar and select one from the list, or go to Microsoft Channel Guide to select from a much larger set. Just follow the instructions and be patient – setting up a channel takes time.

Figure 10.13 The BBC Online Channel. If you connect through a dial-up line, browsing is more efficient than using channels.

10.8 Files from the Net

Shareware sites

One of the great things about the Internet is that you can get from the Net virtually all the tools that you need to work on the Net. You already have a browser, of course, but there are more tools that you may like to acquire. The Internet is also a great source of games, audio and video clips, pictures, text files and more.

If you are looking for software, try these great shareware sites, both run by c|net – shareware.com (**http://www.shareware.com**) and download.com (**http://www.download.com**). Here you can search by keyword or program name, or browse by category. When you find something that you want, clicking on the program's name will start the download – decide which folder to store it in, and sit back and wait. Downloading speeds vary, but average around 100Kb per minute.

Figure 10.14 shareware.com – a great source of software. Some of it is completely free, the rest is shareware – try it for free, but pay a (small) fee to continue using it.

ZIPPED FILES

Many of the files available over the Internet are ZIPped to save space. This can reduce file sizes, and therefore transfer times, by anything from 10% to 90%. You will need **WinZIP** to uncompress them. You can find a copy at shareware.com.

Saving pages and images

You can revisit a page, offline, for as long as it is kept in the temporary files area, but if you want a permanent copy of a page you should save it.

- Wait until the page is fully loaded, then open the **File** menu and select **Save As** – you may need to change the filename to something more memorable.
- When you want to view the page again, use **File → Open**, then browse through your folders to locate it.

Figure 10.15 Saving an image off a Web page. If you like art, try the Web Museum. There are mirror copies of this at many sites, including **http://sunsite.doc.ic.ac.uk/wm**

Only the text of the page will be saved – though this does include all its hyperlinks. If you want the images, each must be saved separately.

■ Right-click on the image and select **Save Picture As** from the short menu. If you have also saved its page, and want the image to be displayed in it, both must be saved in the same folder, and the filename must not be changed. Even then it may not be displayed – it depends on how it was linked. An image can be displayed by itself simply be loading it into a graphics program or Internet Explorer.

Windows Update

You must have noticed the Windows Update shortcuts – on the main **Start** menu, the **Settings** submenu and in the **Links** toolbar. Next time that you are online, click on one of these and go to the Windows Update page. This is a highly automated page. It has routines that will check over your system

Figure 10.16 The Windows Update page. My system has just been checked, and the routine hasn't found any files that need updating. However, while I'm here, I might go and see what's cool or new that I can download for free!

to see if there are any files for which new replacements or 'patch' repairs
are available. If there are any – or if you find any optional add-ons that
you would like – they will be downloaded and installed for you.

Keep at least one of the Windows Update shortcuts, and visit every month
or so to see what's new.

NETSCAPE NAVIGATOR

Internet Explorer is not the only browser! It just happens to be
the one that comes with Windows 98. The Netscape
Corporation produce excellent browsers and other Internet
software. Their latest browser is Navigator, which can be
downloaded by itself or as part of the Communicator
package (with e-mail, newsgroups and other software). Get
it free from:

http://www.netscape.com

Installation is simple, and the software is fast, reliable and easy
to use. If you are going to spend much time on the Internet,
do give their software a try – you may prefer it to Explorer.

10.9 Summary

- The Internet is the result of world-wide cooperation between
  computer networks in commercial, educational and other
  organisations. It is open to all – many millions have already
  joined, and more are joining every day.

- To set up a home terminal, you need a modem, a convenient
  phone line and an account with a service provider. Links to,
  and the software for, some providers are in the Online
  Services folder.

- The Connection Wizard can be used to find a provider, or to
  set up a connection to one where you already have an account.

- Internet Explorer is supplied as part of Windows 98. It exists
  as a separate program, but can be called up from within
  Windows Explorer and My Computer.

- Some of the Internet options should be set early on; others
  can be left until you have spent more time on the Internet.

- If children can get online from your PC, you should enable the Content Advisor, and perhaps install additional child safety software.

- The Web consists of pages linked together by URLs given as hyperlinks in the pages.

- Every site on the Internet has its own unique address – its URL (Uniform Resource Locator). If you know the URL of a page, you can jump directly to it.

- There are places to start browsing from at Microsoft's site.

- Directories help you find your way around; Yahoo is the most comprehensive of these. Search engines can be used to track down pages containing keywords.

- The Explorer Bar can be used to run an online search, or to open the History, Favorites or Channels folders.

- You can add pages to the Favorites folder, and organise them into your own set of folders.

- Files can be downloaded from many places on the Internet – the shareware sites hold stores of free and cheap software.

- A Web page can be saved as a file. If you want its pictures, they must be saved separately.

- Use Windows Update to keep your system up to date.

- Netscape Navigator is an alternative browser and well worth a close look.

11 | OUTLOOK EXPRESS

11.1 Aims of this chapter

If you want to handle e-mail or access the newsgroups, you need suitable software. Windows 98 supplies Outlook Express for this, though if you already have mail and news software installed, you could continue to use that instead. In this chapter we will take a look at the main facilities offered by Outlook Express, and cover some of the key points about e-mail and news in general.

11.2 Starting Outlook Express

Outlook Express can be started from the Desktop icon of the **Programs ➜ Internet Explorer** menu. The initial screen should have the Folder List to the left of the main pane, with its icons for starting the various routines, and the usual toolbar and menu bar above. There are alternative displays – reach them through the **View ➜ Layout** command.

- The **Outlook Bar** can be used as well as, or in place of, the Folder list for moving round the system.
- The **Folder Bar** can be turned on to provide a more substantial heading (it doesn't do anything else).

CONFIGURING MAIL AND NEWS

If you skipped the Mail and News sections of the Connection Wizard when you set up Explorer, they must be dealt with before you can do much with Outlook Express. Click on the Read Mail icon to start the wizard to set up your mail, then click on the Read News icon to run the news wizard.

Outlook Bar   Folder Bar   Folder List

Figure 11.1 The Outlook Express screen, with all optional elements displayed. Use either the Outlook Bar or Folder List to move around the system – you do not need both. The Folder Bar is just decorative.

The Folders

At first, there are only five folders – six if you have the news set up. More can be created as needed to provide organised storage for any mail messages and news articles that you want to retain.

- The **Inbox** holds mail sent to you. The messages remain here, after reading, until you move or delete them.

- The **Outbox** provides temporary storage for messages, while they are waiting to be sent. If you compose your messages offline, you are only online to your service provider for as long as it takes to send them and to collect incoming mail. It doesn't just reduce your costs, it also gives you time to check your text for typing and spelling errors first.

- The **Sent** folder keeps a copy of outgoing messages, if you choose to keep copies (see page 152).

- **Deleted Items** is where messages and articles are stored when they are first deleted. They are only removed completely when deleted from here.
- Use **Drafts** as a temporary store for messages that you want to work on some more before sending.
- If you have set up a news server, you will have a news folder.

11.3 Reading mail

All mail and news folders follow the same pattern. In the top pane there is a list of the message or article headers. These show the name of the sender, its subject and when it was received. They are normally in date order, but can be sorted by sender, subject or date, by clicking on the column name. If the message has not yet been read, its header will be in **bold**. When you select a header, the message is displayed in the preview pane (or in a separate window, if you have chosen this options).

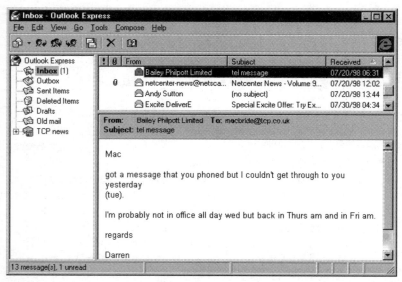

Figure 11.2 The Inbox, with a message in the preview pane. The **View → Columns...** option lets you select which items to display in the headers lines, though *From, Subject* and *Received* are generally enough to be able to find and sort messages efficiently.

When a message is displayed, these tools are available for dealing with it:

Reply – opens the Compose window, with the sender's name in the To: slot, ready to send back to them.

Reply to all – use this instead of Reply where a message has been mailed to a group of people. Your reply will then be mailed to all those who received a **To:** or **Cc:** copy (page 151) of the message.

Forward – copies the message into the Compose window, so that you can send it on to another person.

Delete – moves the message to the Deleted folder.

■ You can also drag a message, at any time, from the header list to another folder for storage.

When people send you mail, it is stored in your mailbox at your Internet service provider.

If you work in an organisation with a permanently open connection to the Internet, you can set up the options (page 151), so that Outlook Express checks the box and downloads new messages for you at set intervals.

If you get online through a dial-up connection, pick up your mail, and send any messages from your Outbox, whenever you are ready.

Use one of the options on the **Tools** menu – **Send** or **Send and Receive** or **Download All** (this will collect your mail and the headers for any newsgroups to which you have subscribed – see page 160).

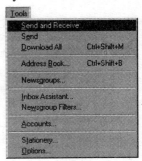

11.4 Sending mail

Outlook Express, like all newer mail software, can handle messages in HTML format (as used on Web pages), as well as plain text. This means that you can use different fonts, sizes and colours for your text, set bulleted or numbered lists and other layout options, and insert pictures. If you want colourful messages, without the bother of formatting them, there are a dozen Stationery styles. These will give you decorative backgrounds and some also have matching text formats already set.

■ Don't waste time formatting messages if the person to whom you are writing can only read plain text on their system.

To write and send a message:

1 Click the **Compose** button, or use **Compose → New Message**.

or

1 Open the Compose drop-down list, or select **Compose → New Message Using** and pick your Stationery from the list.

If you decide you don't like the chosen Stationery, **Format → Apply Stationery** will let you choose another style, or revert to a plain background.

2 When the Compose window opens, either type the recipient's e-mail address into the **To**: box, or click **To**: and select it from your Address Book (see page 153 for more on this).

3 If more than one person is to get a copy, you can add addresses in the **To**: box (separated by semicolons or commas), or put them in the **Cc**: or **Bcc**: boxes.

Figure 11.3 Composing a message using the Balloon Party Stationery – apply formats as in a normal word-processing.

To: the main recipients – you would normally expect replies from these people.

Cc: Carbon copies, sent mainly for information.

Bcc: Blind carbon copies – their names will not appear in the lists of recipients that normally accompany each message. Used for circulating mail to large groups.

4 Type a **Subject** for your message, so that your recipients will know what the message is about when they see the header line in their mail window.

5 Type and format your message.

6 Click the **Send** button. The message will either be sent immediately, or stored in the Outbox to be sent later – it depends on your settings (page 152).

or

6 Open the **File** menu and select **Send Message** (i.e. now) or **Send Later** to override your option setting.

11.5 Outlook Express options

As with most software, the optional settings make more sense after you have been using it for a while, and the default settings are usually a safe bet to start with. However, there are a few that are worth checking and setting early on. Use **Tools ➔ Options...** to open the **Options** panel.

The **General** tab deals with the interaction between Outlook Express and your system.

■ Turn on '*Check for new messages every ?? minutes*', and set the interval, if you are permanently online or have long online sessions.

■ Turn off '*Notify me if there are any new newsgroups*' if you don't bother much with the news.

■ Turning on '*Automatically put people I reply to in my Address Book*' is a good idea. It ensures that their address is correct – as it has been copied from their mail. If this includes some people you do not want, they can easily be removed.

■ All the other options are probably best turned on at this stage.

The **Send** tab is mainly about message formats, see Figure 11.4.

Will most of your recipients be able to read **HTML** formatted messages?

News articles are best left as **Plain Text**

Keep a copy of the messages you send?

It's useful to include the original message in your reply – you can edit out the bits you don't want.

Turn on **Send immediately** if you normally deal with your mail online.

Figure 11.4 The **Send** options.

The **Read** tab is mainly concerned with news articles.

- Some groups have 100s of articles every day. You can set how many headers to download at a time.
- Where a set of articles has the same Subject (follow-ons are prefaced by 'Re:') they are known as a thread. If the **Automatically expand threads** option is off, only the first is shown until you click ⊞ to expand it.

The **Security** tab should be left alone for the time being – and can be ignored altogether if you are not bothered about the security of your mail.

On the **Advanced** tab the main question is how long – if at all – do you want to keep old newsgroup articles? Remember that selected messages can be copied to other folders for storage. The **Logging** options can be turned on if you have problems with your mail or news. The log files could provide useful information for whoever tries to solve the problems.

If you intend running Outlook Express while you are already online with Internet Explorer, select **Do not dial...** and turn off **Hang up when finished...**

Figure 11.5 Suitable settings for handling your mail separately from browsing. You may want to compose messages before going online to send and receive. Automatic hang up will save your phone bills.

11.6 The Address Book

You must get e-mail addresses exactly right, or the post won't get through. Unfortunately, addresses are not always user-friendly and are rarely easy to remember. The Address Book is a great idea. Once you have an e-mail address in here – correctly – you need never worry about it again. When you want to write to someone, you can select the name from the book and start to compose from there, or start the message and then select the names at the **To:** and **Cc:** boxes (see page 151).

Adding to the Address Book

1 Open the **Address Book** from the **Tools** menu.
2 Click the **New Contact** tool. The **Properties** panel has tabs for lots of different contact information. The only one that is essential is the **Personal** tab.

Figure 11.6 My Address Book – lots more to add yet! It is handy to keep phone numbers here as well.

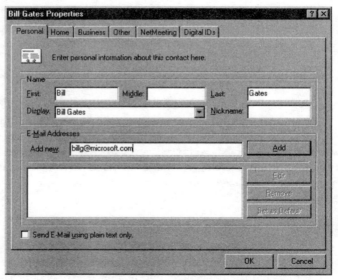

Figure 11.7 Adding a new contact. First and last names and the address are the only essentials, and are quickly added.

3 The First, Middle and Last names should be entered separately if you want to be able to sort the list by First and Last names. (**View → Sort By** has a number of alternative sort orders – very useful when you have lots of entries.)

4 A **Nickname** can be entered, if wanted, and either this or the full name can be set as the **Display** value.

5 Type the address *carefully* into the **Add new:** box, and click **Add**. If the person has more than one e-mail address, add the others then select one as the default.

6 If you know that the person can only handle plain text on their system. turn on **Send E-mail using plain text only**.

7 Switch to the other tabs to enter more details if required, then click **OK**.

COPYING E-MAIL ADDRESSES

If you have received an e-mail from someone that you want to add to the Address Book, the address can be copied in almost automatically. Start to reply to the person, then right-click on the name in the To: slot. Select **Add To Address Book** from the short menu. The name and e-mail address will be copied into the appropriate places for you. If you don't actually want to reply to them at that time, just close down the Compose window to cancel the reply.

Using the Address Book

If the Address Book is open already, you can start a new message to someone by selecting their name and clicking the **Send Mail** button. The **Compose** window will open, with the name in the **To:** box.

If you start from the Compose button, click the ▤ icon to open the **Select Recipients** panel. This lists the names in your Address Book. Pick the names of the recipients one at a time, clicking **To->**, **Cc->** or **Bcc->** to copy them to the appropriate categories. Click **OK** to return to the Compose window.

The recipients will appear as names, rather than e-mail addresses – don't worry. They will be translated into addresses before sending.

If you add a name
by mistake, just
select it and press
the **Delete** key.

Figure 11.8 Using the **Select Recipients** panel to get addresses from
your Address Book.

11.7 Finding people

The simplest and safest way to get someone's e-mail address is to ring
them up and ask them to send you e-mail. If this isn't possible, you may be
able to find the address in one of the Internet's people-finding sites. These
hold databases of names and addresses that they have compiled in various
ways – none give a complete coverage. You are more likely to be able to
find someone if they get online through a service provider than if they
connect through a business or other organisation – these are often reluctant
to release internal information to the people-finding databases. If you are
looking for people in the USA, you can probably find their phone numbers
easier than their e-mail addresses, as most of the sites have the US telephone
databases. Having said all that, it's always worth a try. You may be able to
find that long-lost schoolchum, or Uncle Arthur who emigrated in 1964.

You can run a search at half a dozen of the best sites through the **Find
People** panel.

    1 Go online.

    2 Pick a site from the **Look in** list – it doesn't matter which.

    3 Type in the first and last names.

4 Click **Find Now**.

5 If it doesn't work, try different sites. If you still have no joy, try with just the initial and the name – you cannot be sure how they gave their name when they signed up for e-mail. This will produce more unwanted hits for you to sort through.

6 If your search produces too many results, you may be better going to the Web site – click the button to connect to the current **Look in** site. Most have advanced search facilities that will let you define your search more closely.

Figure 11.9 Starting a search for an e-mail address. If InfoSpace has a 'Tony Blair' in its database, the panel will expand to show the results.

11.8 Newsgroups

Newsgroups are where people come together to share common interests and enthusiasms, to ask for and to give help, to debate and to announce new discoveries and creations. There are over 20,000 of them, each devoted to a different topic, ranging from the seriously academic to the totally trivial. They are organised into about 20 major (and many more minor) divisions, subdivided by topic, and subdivided again where necessary.

Their names reflect this structure and describe their focus; thus, for example, rec.arts.animation is found in the arts sub-division of the rec main division and is devoted to animation as an art form. (There are other animation groups, with different focuses.)

Most newsgroups belong to one or other of these divisions.

alt – the alternative newsgroups, set up to cover topics that had not been included in the other main divisions. Hobbies, obsessions and fan clubs form a substantial part of the **alt** groups, though there are also groups for professional interests and discussions. As a neat example of the diversity, here are three adjacent groups: *alt.architecture.int-design*, *alt.aromatherapy*, *alt.art.bodypainting*.

biz – business-oriented groups, carrying announcements of new products, job opportunities and discussions of market-related issues.

comp – a large set of newsgroups covering many aspects of computing, including languages, applications, hardware and standards.

misc – miscellaneous. Books, health, education, kids, for sale adverts and job opportunities make up the bulk of these.

news – amongst these newsgroups about newsgroups you will find several specially for new users. *news.newusers* is a good source of tips and advice, while *news.answers* may solve your problems.

rec – a very large set covering the whole range of recreational activities from arts through games to sports, with virtually everything in between. These three give an idea of the diversity: *rec.arts.sf.tv.quantum-leap*, *rec.games.xtank.programmer*, *rec.gardens.orchids*.

sci – academic and professional scientific discussion groups.

soc – most of the groups here are for discussions of different cultures, religions and social issues.

MODERATION

Some newsgroups are *moderated* – they have someone to check articles and weed out the irrelevant ones. Moderation is not really necessary for specialised academic or professional groups, as the quantity of articles tends to be low – and the quality high. With popular newsgroups – those devoted to TV shows, pop stars, sports or anything to do with sex – moderation is more needed and frequently absent. They tend to generate huge numbers of articles – and the quality is highly variable.

11.9 Reading the news

Outlook Express offers a simple but effective routine for finding and sampling or subscribing to newsgroups.

1 Go to the news folder and click the **Newsgroups** button on the main window to open the panel shown below.

2 Type a word, or part of a word, into the **Display newsgroups which contain** box. The list is filtered to display only those groups whose names contain the given letters.

3 When you see a group that looks interesting, select it and click **Go to**. (Or if you see a group that you know you want to read regularly, click **Subscribe**.) You will be returned to the main Outlook screen, with the selected group active.

4 If, after sampling its articles, you decide that you would like to add the group to your subscribed list, right click on it and select **Subscribe** from the short menu.

Figure 11.10 Finding newsgroups. A simple keyword search will usually produce a good selection. Collect the list of new groups from your service provider, from time to time. Initially they wil be listed on the **New** tab – use **Reset list** to move them to the **All** list after you've had chance to look through to see if you fancy any.

SUBSCRIBING TO GROUPS

If you subscribe to a group, it is added to your news folder so
you don't have to go and find it every time. You can also
download the headers for any new articles in your subscribed
groups using **Tools → Download All**.

Headers and articles

A newsgroup may generate hundreds of new articles every day. Even if
you are fascinated by the topic of the newsgroup, you are unlikely to want
to read every article. Read the Subjects in the headers in the top pane to
find the nature of the articles, and whether or not you want to read them.

If you want to respond to an article, either send an e-mail to the author
only, or post a follow-up article to the group. In general, if the original
article was a request for information, reply to the author.

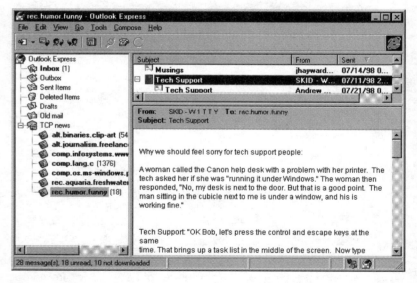

Figure 11.11 Reading the news. Select a newsgroup and download
the headers, and select from there to download and read articles.

If you want to **follow up** on an article with your own contribution to the discussion, you would normally quote the relevant lines from the original article or give a brief summary of the key points that you want to pick up.

If you want to put out your own request for information, or to start a new discussion, then you **post** your article to the group.

Don't rush into posting articles. There are few things existing members find more irritating than a 'newbie' asking obvious questions or rehearsing old arguments. Spend some time 'lurking' – reading without posting – to pick up the true flavour of the group and find out what topics have been discussed recently. You should also track down the group's Frequently Asked Questions list.

NEWSGROUP NETIQUETTE

Like much of the rest of the Internet the newsgroup system relies on cooperation, voluntary labour, some sponsorship and a set of agreed rules – its *Netiquette*. Take the trouble to learn the rules and use them. Using Netiquette is not just about being a good news user – it is also a matter of self-preservation. The thing to remember is that, with a popular group, an article may be downloaded by several thousand people, and many of these will be paying phone and on-line charges to get it. If you waste their time and money, they will not be happy and may well respond with *flames* – angry mail.

11.10 Summary

- Outlook Express handles mail and news through a set of folders. The key ones are the Inbox, where incoming mail is stored, the Outbox, where mail is held before sending, and the newsgroups folder.

- The subjects in the header lines should give you an idea of the nature of a message. You can easily reply to, or forward on, incoming mail.

- When composing a new message, you can use Stationery and apply formats to the text.

- Messages can be sent immediately, or stored for transmission later when you go online.
- The Options control your interaction with the system, and how and when messages are sent and read. Some options are more for newsgroups than e-mail.
- Use the Address Book to store the e-mail addresses of your contacts, and you will only have to type an address once!
- The Find People facility enables you to search some of the main people databases on the Internet.
- Newsgroups allow people from all over the world to share common interests and problems.
- There are over 20,000 newsgroups and mailing lists, covering almost every aspect of human (and alien!) life.
- Some groups generate huge numbers of articles – and of variable quality! You can go to a group to sample its contents, or subscribe if you intend reading regularly.
- Outlook Express has a good routine for finding groups, and lets you dip into them without subscribing.
- If you post articles to newsgroups, observe the Netiquette!

WANT TO KNOW MORE?

If you want to know more about using e-mail and the newsgroups, try *Teach Yourself the Internet*.

---

12 | MAINTAINING YOUR DISKS

12.1 Aims of this chapter

Today's hard disks should give you years of trouble-free service. They will, however, give better service if they are maintained properly. Windows 98 has tools that do all the donkey work, once you have started them off – you can even set them up so that they run automatically. Hard disks are now far more reliable than they were only a few years ago – it's unusual for them to become corrupted and lose data, even rarer to crash altogether. But these things do happen, and files can become corrupted through software errors or lost through human error. For all these reasons, it is important to protect your valuable data by backing it up regularly.

Floppy disks are more variable in quality, but reliable if treated properly. Initial formatting and checking, and careful storage is more important than regular maintenance for floppies.

12.2 The System Tools

These can all be reached from the **Start** menu, through **Programs → Accessories → System Tools**. As well as the ones that we will be covering in this chapter, you may also find these tools:

Compression Agent

This is only relevant for machines which have been upgraded from earlier versions of Windows. The space on disks is divided into clusters. When a file is written to the disk, it is stored in a linked set of clusters, filling each in turn until it reaches the last where there will, inevitably, be some spare space. The next file to be written will then go into the next unused cluster. Earlier Windows PCs used the FAT16 (16-bit File Allocation Table) system, with a cluster, or allocation unit, size of 16Kb (on a 1Mb drive), which left

Figure 12.1 The **System Tools** menu. You may well have a slightly different set, but if they do not include Backup, Disk Cleanup, Disk Defragmenter and Scandisk, run the Windows Setup again and install the missing tools.

anything up to 15.99Kb wasted space at the end of each file. Windows 98 PCs use FAT32, with much smaller clusters. If you have upgraded, you can convert your drive to FAT32, to make more efficient use of disk space. This is not essential. Windows 98 can work quite happily with FAT16, though earlier versions cannot cope with FAT32. If there is any possibility that you might want to revert back to Windows 95 or 3.1, do not convert!

DriveSpace

Largely irrelevant on new Windows 98 PCs, DriveSpace can compress FAT16 (but not FAT32) disks to give more storage space. It was developed when hard disks were relatively small, and boosting them from, say, 100Mb to nearly 200Mb was worth the slight loss of performance – compression slows down reading and writing. Most PCs now have hard disks of at least 2Mb – far more than most people will need – so compression is less needed. It is worth thinking about if you need to get a large file onto a floppy, but even here, you may be better off compressing the file with WinZip (see page 142) and storing it on a normal floppy.

12.3 Disk Properties

If you right-click on a drive in Explorer or My Computer, and select Properties from the menu, the Properties panel will open.

- The **General** tab shows how much used and free space you have on the drive.
- The **Tools** tab has buttons to start ScanDisk, Backup and Disk Defragmenter.
- The **Sharing** tab is only present if you are on a network.
- The **Compression** tab is only there if DriveSpace can be used.

This runs ScanDisk

Figure 12.2 The **Properties** panel for a C: drive.

DISKS AND DRIVES

These words are often used interchangeably, and for some purposes they are effectively the same. Strictly speaking, a disk is that flat, round thing on which data is stored, while a drive is a logical area of storage identified by a letter (A:, C:, etc). The A: drive can have different disks put into it. A hard disk can be partitioned to create two or more drives.

12.4 Disk Cleanup

This is the simplest of the system tools, and one that should be run fairly regularly to free up space. It removes temporary and other unwanted files from the hard disk. When you start Disk Cleanup, the first job is to select the drive – normally **C:**. You then select the sets of files to delete.

- **Temporary Internet Files** – don't remove these if you want to be able to revisit pages without having to go online and download them again.
- **Downloaded Program Files** refer to Java or ActiveX applets (small programs) that you met on Web pages, and had to be stored on your disk so that they could be run.
- **Recycle Bin** – this just saves you having to empty the Bin as a separate operation.
- **Temporary files** refers to those created by applications – typically automatic backups and print files. They are normally cleaned up when the application is closed, but may be left behind especially if it ends with a crash. Disk Cleanup will not touch new files, which the application may still be using.

After you have made your selection and clicked **OK**, you will be prompted to confirm the deletions – they are irreversible – before the cleanup starts.

12.5 ScanDisk

ScanDisk will find and fix errors on a disk. It can be run at two levels.

- A **Standard** scan checks that all files and folders are where they are supposed to be on the disk. This is the one that you would normally use, and takes only a few minutes.

Figure 12.3 Disk Cleanup. The **More Options** tab takes you to Add/ Remove programs; on **Settings** you can opt to run Disk Cleanup automatically if you get short of space.

- ■ A **Thorough** scan also checks that the disk surface is sound, and that data can be written to and read from it correctly. Use this when first checking a disk, after significant errors have been shown by a Standard check, and as part of an occasional overhaul of your system. It takes up to an hour to run on a hard disk – start it, then go and do something useful.

If the **fix errors** option is turned on, ScanDisk will move data from dodgy areas of the disk – if it finds any – and store it more safely elsewhere.

The **Advanced Options** apply to all scans. The key options here are:
- ■ **Lost file fragments** – data-filled clusters that are no longer linked to their files. They can be converted to files (named FILE001.CHK, FILE002.CHK, etc, and stored in C:\). If the data is text it may be possible to recover it from here by opening the files in a word-processor. Other forms of data are generally not recoverable.

■ **Cross-linked files** – where the same data is linked to two
files. The data can only belong to one of the two – and may,
in fact, belong to neither. Making a copy may leave one of
the files intact.

Files in the System area
cannot normally be moved
– they must be at set
locations. If there are errors
here, its time for a new disk.

This only applies
to **Thorough**.

'Host drive' only applies
to DriveSpace disks

Figure 12.4 Setting the **ScanDisk** options.

ScanDisk Results - [C:]

ScanDisk did not find any errors on this drive.

852,328,448 bytes total disk space
0 bytes in bad sectors
4,734,976 bytes in 287 folders
32,784,384 bytes in 208 hidden files
367,083,520 bytes in 4,289 user files
447,725,568 bytes available on disk

16,384 bytes in each allocation unit
52,022 total allocation units on disk
27,327 available allocation units

Close

Figure 12.5 ScanDisk has given this drive a clean bill of health. To a certain extent, 'bad sectors' do not matter – ScanDisk will mark them off so that Windows does not try to store data there. If you have a high proportion of bad sectors – over 5% or so – throw a floppy disk away and think about replacing a hard drive.

12.6 Disk Defragmenter

We noted earlier that the storage space on a disk is divided into clusters, and that a file may occupy any number of clusters, each linked to the next. On a new, clean disk, each file will normally be written in a set of clusters that are physically continuous on the disk. Over time, as the disk fills up, and as files are written, rewritten (larger or smaller) and deleted, it gradually becomes more difficult to store files in adjacent clusters – the disk is becoming *fragmented*. The files are still safe, but they cannot be read as quickly if the reading heads have to hop all over the disk.

Disk Defragmenter reorganises the physical storage of files on the disk, pulling together the data from scattered clusters. Though it improves performance, the gains are in the order of a few seconds for starting a program or loading a data file, and it is a very slow job – allow an hour on a 2Mb disk. It is only worth doing regularly if your disk is almost full – so that new files are being stored in a limited area – or if you have a high turnover of files from working on large databases or reports, or from installing and removing demos, shareware and other programs.

1 If any other program writes to the disk while Disk Defragmenter is running, it will restart from scratch. Shut down any applications that may write temporary files to the disk. You should also open the Desktop's **Properties** panel and turn off the screensaver. This may also write to the disk.

2 Start Disk Defragmenter from the **System Tools** menu.

Select the drive, then check the **Settings** before starting

The job will take ages anyway, so you may as well do it properly!

It's worth watching Defragmenter at work – for a little while – just to see what it does.

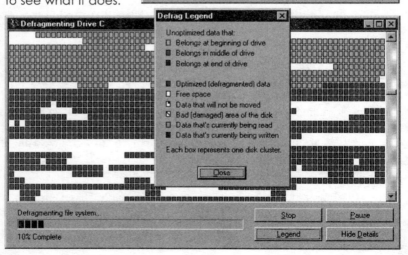

Figure 12.6 Defragmenting the drive – a slow job, but worth doing when the drive starts to fill.

3 Select the drive and click the **Options** button.

   If you have scanned the disk recently, you can clear the **check for errors** option to save a little time.

4 Click the **Show Details** button if you want to see what's going on, then turn on the **Legend** so that you can understand it!

5 When you get bored, go and do something else for an hour.

RESTORING CORRUPTED FLOPPIES

If a floppy disk becomes corrupted so that you cannot read its files, try running it through ScanDisk then Disk Defragmenter, It doesn't take long to process a floppy and it will sometimes recover the lost files.

12.7 Windows Tune-Up

You can set up Disk Cleanup, ScanDisk and Disk Defragmenter to run automatically at set times – in fact, they may already have been set up when Windows 98 was installed. Whether you are doing it for the first time, or checking and adjusting the settings, use Windows Tune-Up or Maintenance Wizard (both shortcuts lead to the same point).

Use this option if your system needs an immediate full service – it's simpler than starting the three utilities separately.

1 When the Wizard opens, select **Change my maintenance settings...** and Click **OK**.

2 At the first panel, select **Express** if you are happy to let Windows 98 make your decisions, or **Custom** if you would like to see – and control – what's going on.

3 Pick a convenient time for maintenance – it must be when you will not be using the machine. If you have chosen the Express route, click **Finish**, otherwise click **Next**.

Remember that **Cleanup** and the standard **ScanDisk** only take a few minutes.

4 If there are any programs in your Startup folder – i.e. ones that run automatically when Windows starts – you will be asked if you want to run them.

5 You will see a panel for each of Disk Defragmenter, ScanDisk and DiskCleanup. All follow the same format. If you choose to run the utility, you can change when and how often it runs by clicking **Reschedule**, and set its options by clicking **Settings** – this leads to the utility's normal options panel.

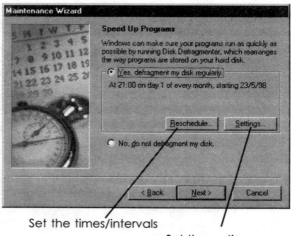

The tools can be run at different times and intervals – and you can run just one or two.

Set the times/intervals

Set the options

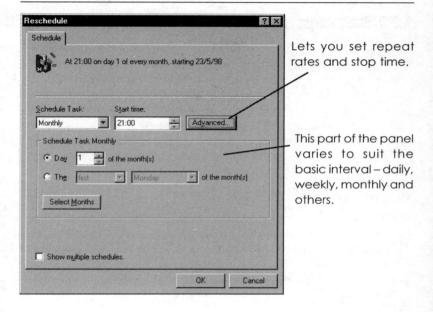

Lets you set repeat rates and stop time.

This part of the panel varies to suit the basic interval – daily, weekly, monthly and others.

Scheduled Tasks

After the Maintenance Wizard has been run, the settings are stored in the **Scheduled Tasks** folder. This can be opened from the **System Tools** menu. Click on an icon here to enable or disable a task, or to change its schedule or settings.

If you have another program that you want to run regularly, at set times, click here to set it up as a scheduled task.

Figure 12.7 The **Scheduled Tasks** folder. Running a Tune-up icon simply opens its configuration panel – it does not start the tasked program.

12.8 Backup

If an application's program files become corrupted or accidentally deleted, it is a nuisance but not a major problem as you can simply reinstall the application from the original disks. Data files are a different matter. How much is your data worth to you? How long would it take you to rewrite that report, redraw that picture or re-enter the last six months' accounts if they were lost? Individual files can be copied onto floppies for safekeeping, but if you have more than one or two it is simpler to use Backup. A backup job is easily set up, doesn't take long to run and will more than pay for itself in time and trouble the first time that you need it!

Backup media

Backups can be done on floppy disks, and this is fine for home use or in a small business where there's not a lot to backup – with compression, over 2Mb of data will fit on one disk. If you intend to backup large quantities of data regularly, invest £100 or so in a tape drive or an IOmega removable hard disk system – it will be far easier than struggling with a pile of floppies.

Whatever you save on must be removable. You must be able to store the backup away from the machine – in a fireproof safe or a different building if you want real security.

The Backup Wizard

When you start Backup, you will be asked if you want to create a new backup, use an existing job or restore files. The **create** option will start a Wizard to guide you through it. (After the first few times, you may prefer to set it up directly, in which case, click **Cancel** to close the Wizard.)

1 At the first stage, if you want to do a full backup – of everything on your system – select **Back up My Computer**. This is not a viable option if you are backing up on floppy disks!

2 If you opt to back up selected files and folders, you will be given an Explorer-style display. Click the ⊞ icons to open out the folders as necessary.

   Simply tick a folder if you want to back up everything in it.

   To select items within a folder, click on its name to open it, then tick individual items.

If you select a folder, all its contents are selected – clear the checkboxes for those that you do not want to back up.

3 At the next stage, you can opt to back up all files, or only those that are new or have changed since the previous backup. Using the 'new and changed' option here can save you having to select individual files from folders at the previous stage.

4 Select the medium (tape, disk, etc) and drive if saving to disk.

5 There are two options: **Compare original and backup to verify...** , and **Compress...** – both are best turned on.

6 At the final stage, you need to give your backup job a name – this should describe the file selection and the date.

Backup Job Options

If you create your backup job from within Backup, you have more control than through the Wizard. Use **Job → Options** to open the **Options** panel.

- The **General** options are the same as in the Wizard – turn on Compare and Compress if wanted.

- On the **Password** tab you can protect your files with password.

- On the **Type** tab, you can choose to backup *All selected files*, as in the Wizard, or *new and changed only*. This can be done in two ways. A **Differential** backup will save those files that have changed since last 'All files' operation; an **Incremental** backup saves those changed since last the 'All files' or Incremental backup. The Incremental is smaller, but restoring files can be simpler and quicker from a Differential backup.

- The **Exclude** tab allows you to choose File Types to exclude from all backups – if there are types which you know that you don't mind losing (such as decorative stuff from Web pages) – list them here. It's a slow job, as each type must be added separately.

Figure 12.8 The **Backup Job Options** panel, open at the **Exclude** tab. Click **Add** to open a list of File Types – you can only add one at a time, but the list is retained.

■ On the **Report** tab, select items to include in the report after the job is done. This tab has a useful **Perform an unattended backup** option – turn this on if you are not going to be on hand to respond to any messages and prompts as it runs.

■ On the **Advanced** tab, turn on **Back up Windows Registry** to ensure that it is saved if the Windows folder is selected.

Restoring files

With any luck this will never be necessary! But if you do have to do it, at least it is not difficult.

1 Run Backup, and select **Restore** at the opening panel.
2 Insert the disk or tape with the backup into its drive.
3 Select the backup set, then click **Refresh** to update the display.
4 Open the folders as necessary until you can see the files and folders that you want to restore. Tick to select them.
5 Click **Start** – that's it.

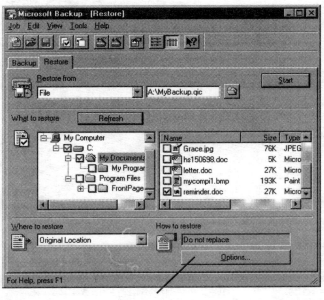

If a file is present on the computer, it is not normally replaced. Change this option if you want to overwrite a file with its older, backup version.

12.9 Floppy disks

These are mainly used for backups and for copying files from one computer to another. Before use they will need formatting – unless you have bought them ready-formatted.

1 Place an unformatted disk in the floppy drive.

2 Right-click on the **A:** icon in My Computer or Explorer and select **Format** from the menu.

3 In **Format Type**, select *Full*. A *Quick* format will erase files from a formatted disk; *Copy system files* is used to create a startup disk.

4 Type a **Label** if wanted – the paper label is more use for identifying floppies.

5 Click **Start**.

Formatting destroys all the data on a disk. **Do not format the C: drive!** The option exists, but should only be used as a last ditch attempt to recover something from the ruins of a major virus attack or other total failure, or before installing a new (non-Windows) operating system.

FLOPPY CARE

Floppies are quite robust, but their files can be corrupted if exposed to heat or magnetism. Keep them away from radiators, magnets, heavy machinery and electricity cables.

12.10 Summary

- Hard disks need regular maintenance to keep them in good condition. Windows 98 provides tools for this.

- The maintenance utilities can be started from the System Tools menu, or from the Tools tab of the Disk Properties panel.

- Disk Cleanup will remove temporary and unwanted files.

- Use ScanDisk regularly to check that your files and folders are intact and correctly stored. Run it in Thorough mode occasionally to check the condition of the disk surface.

- Disk Defragmenter will reorganise the disk so that files are stored in continuous sequences for faster reading.

- Windows Tune-Up simplifies maintenance. With its wizard you can arrange for the maintenance tools to be run at set times as scheduled tasks.

- If you do not want to lose important data, it should be backed up. If files are corrupted or deleted, they can then be restored.

- Floppies must be formatted before use.

13 PRINTERS

13.1 Aims of this chapter

With Windows 98, much hardware is simply plug and play – just connect it up, and Windows will configure the system so that the new kit is ready to run. Printers are a little bit different. If you want to get the best out of your printer, you must use the right driver – the program that converts the computer's formatting codes into ones that the printer understands. And there will almost certainly be the right driver for your printer, as there are over 1,000 on the Windows CD. In this chapter we will look at how to install a new printer, and how to control it in use.

13.2 Adding a new printer

If your printer model dates from before Spring 1998, the drivers on the Windows 98 CD are probably newer than those supplied with the printer. If the printer is more recent, dig out its installation disk.

If there's any kind of technical job to be done, you can be reasonably sure that there will be a wizard to handle it.

1 Open the **Printers** folder, either from **My Computer** or on the **Start → Settings** menu.

2 Click (or double-click) **Add Printer** to run the wizard.

This system has two printers already – the local DeskJet is the default (shown by ●); the Brother is on the network.

3 At the first screen, select *Local printer*, if it is attached directly to your PC, or *Network printer* if you access it through your office Local Area Network.

4 If you are using one of the Windows 98 drivers, select the **Manufacturer** from the list, then the **Printer** model. If you are using those supplied with the printer, click **Have Disk**, then select the model from the list that is drawn from the disk.

Use the printer's own drivers?

5 For a local printer, you need to choose the port – normally LPT1. If you have a (rare) serial printer, use a COM port – COM4 may be free.

Normally used to connect the mouse and modem.

FILE is used if you are outputting files for remote printing, e.g. at a commercial printers.

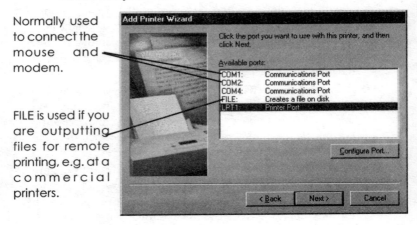

6   For a network printer, browse the network to find the printer
    you want to use.

7   You may want to edit the full manufacturer/model name into
    something shorter to label the icon in the Printers folder.

8   If you have more than one printer, one is set as the default –
    the one that applications will use unless you specify otherwise
    when you start a print job.

9   At the final stage, accept the offer of a test print – it's as well
    to check! Once you click **Finish**, the Wizard will load the
    driver from the disk and install it in your system.

13.3 Printer Properties

Before you use the printer, check its properties. If nothing else, you may
well need to change the paper size, as it is often set to the US 'Letter'. The
standard UK paper size is A4 (210 x 297mm).

Right-click on the new icon in the Printers folder and select **Properties**.
Different printers have different Properties panels, but you should find:

■ A **General** tab, where you can type a comment. This is only
   useful on a network, to inform others of any special
   requirements that you or the printer have.

■ A **Details** tab, where you can select a new port or driver if
   needed. The **Timeout** settings define how long Windows
   should wait before reporting an error; the **Spool** settings
   determine whether the file is sent directly from the application
   to the printer, or through a temporary memory buffer.
   Spooling frees up applications, as they can generally send
   data out faster than the printer can handle it.

■ A **Paper** tab, where you can set the default paper size. The
   other options here are best left at their defaults, though you
   may well want to change them just before printing specific
   documents – the printer properties can be accessed from the
   Print routines of applications.

■ A **Device Options** panel. Check the **Memory** value
   (normally only with laser printers). If you have added extra
   memory to the printer – a good idea if you print pages with
   lots of graphics – tell Windows about it.

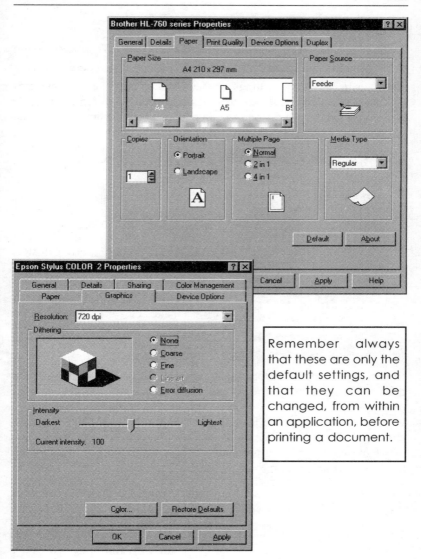

Remember always that these are only the default settings, and that they can be changed, from within an application, before printing a document.

Figure 13.1 The **Properties** panels for two printers. Take time to explore yours to see what options are available, and what defaults have been set – not all may make sense at first!

13.4 Printing from applications

The Print routines in applications are all much the same. There will usually be a ⌨ toolbar button, and clicking on this will send the document to the printer using its current settings – whatever they are. The first time that you print something, it is best to start by selecting **Print** from the **File** menu. This will open a dialog box where you can define the settings – the key ones are which pages to print and how many copies.

With **Collate** on, printing takes longer, but you don't have to sort it afterwards.

Figure 13.2 The Print dialog box from Word. Other applications have different options, but **Page range** and **Copies** are common to all.

If you need to change the layout, print quality or other printer settings, clicking the Properties button will open the printer Properties panel – this may look slightly different from the panel opened from the Printers folder, but gives you access to the same settings.

13.5 Controlling the print queue

Unless you are exceptionally disorganised or have very unreliable hardware, most of your printing will run smoothly. But things go wrong even at the most organised desk...

When a document is sent for printing, it goes first to the print queue. If it is the only print job, it is then processed directly. If not, it will sit in the queue and wait its turn. As long as a document is still in the queue, you can do something about it – but if it is just one short, simple document, it will almost certainly be through the queue before you can get to it.

■ If you discover a late error, so that printing is just a waste of paper, a job can be cancelled.

■ If you have sent a series of documents in succession, you can change the order in which they are printed.

When the printer is active, you will see on the right of the Taskbar, next to the clock. Click on it to open the printer's folder, where the queue is stored.

■ *To cancel a print job*, select the document, then use **Cancel Printing** from the **Document** menu.

■ *To cancel all the queued jobs*, use **Purge Printing** from the **Printer** menu.

■ *To change the order of printing*, select a document and drag it up or down the queue as required – this only works with those documents that are not already being spooled or printed.

DON'T JUST TURN OFF!

Turning off the printer is not a good way to stop a print job. If the document is partially printed or still waiting in the queue it will simply start to print again as soon as the printer is turned back on – and if partially printed, will be probably be garbled. You must clear the queue to get rid of a print job.

13.6 Printing from file

If you have Explorer or My Computer open, you can print a document directly from there, as long as you have an associated application which can handle it. Windows 98 will open the application, print the document, then close the application for you.

To send the document to the default printer:

- Right-click on the file and select **Print** from the short menu.

To send to any other printer:

1 Open the printers folder and arrange the screen so that you can see the document file and the printer icon.

2 Drag the document across the screen and drop it onto the printer icon.

Figure 13.3 You can print a document directly from file, either from the short menu or by dropping it onto a printer icon.

13.7 Summary

- To install a new printer, use the Add Printer wizard in the Printers folder. Windows 98 has drivers for almost every known printer model.

- Check the printer's Properties panel before use, to make sure that the default settings – especially the Paper size – are suitable.

- When printing from an application, you can usually set the page range and number of copies. If required, the printer Properties can be adjusted before printing.

- Documents are taken to the print queue before output. By opening the queue you can cancel a print job or change the order in which they are printed.

- A document can be printed from Explorer or My Computer.

14 THE ACCESSORIES

14.1 Aims of this chapter

The Windows 98 package includes a host of accessories – some very useful, others just for fun. In this chapter we will be looking at a selection of these. Even if you never use any of these accessories in earnest, it is worth experimenting with them, as the skills and knowledge that you learn here can be applied to other Windows applications.

14.2 WordPad

Don't underrate WordPad just because it's free. It has all the facilities that you would have found in the top-flight software of just a few years ago, and compares well with today's commercial packages. It's fine for writing letters, essays, reports, source code for computer programs and anything else where you want to be able to enter and edit text efficiently, formatting it in different fonts, styles and colours, and perhaps incorporating graphics or other files.

- When entering text, just keep typing when you reach the edge of the page – the text will be wrapped round to the next line. Only press the **Enter** key at the end of a paragraph.

- Existing text can be selected, with the normal techniques, then moved, deleted or formatted.

- Most formatting can be done through the toolbar. Select the text, then pick a font or size from the drop-down lists, or click the **B** bold, **I** italic, **U** underline, colour or other buttons.

- The left, centre and right alignment buttons determine how the text lines up with the edges of the paper.

Standard toolbar – with the main filing and editing tools

Formatting toolbar   Ruler

WordPad

Don't underrate WordPad just because it's free. It has all the facilities that you would have found in the top-flight software of just a few years ago, and compares well with today's commercial packages. It's fine for writing letters, essays, reports, source code for computer programs and anything else where you want to be able to enter and edit text efficiently, formatting it in different fonts, styles and colours, and perhaps incorporating graphics or other files.

- When entering text, just keep typing when you reach the edge of the page - the text will be wrapped round to the next line. Only press the Enter key at the end of a paragraph.
- Existing text can be selected, with the normal techniques, then moved, deleted or formatted.
- Most formatting can be done through the toolbar. Select the text, then pick a font or size from the drop-down lists, or click the ▣ bold, ◩ italic, 🖉 colour or other

Figure 14.1 WordPad, being used to create the text for these pages!

- The ▤ bullets button indents text from the left, with a blob at the start of each paragraph.
- These formats apply to whole paragraphs. You do not need to select the whole paragraph – if the cursor is within it, or part of its text is selected, the paragraph will be formatted.

Indents and tabs

These are best set from the ruler. Select the text where new indents or tabs are required then drag the icons to set the indent; click to set a tab point.

Left margin   Right margin
    First line indent   Right indent
                            Tab

Left indent

Full font formatting

Though you can set almost all font options from the toolbar buttons, you get better control through the **Font** panel – open it with **Format ➜ Font**. Here you can set all aspects of the selected text, and preview the effects of your choices. Watch the **Sample** text as you change the settings.

Figure 14.2 The **Font** panel. Click **OK** when you like the look of the **Sample**.

You will find similar panels in all applications that use fonts.

Page Setup

The **Page Setup** panel, opened from the **File** menu option, controls the basic size and layout of the page – for all pages in the document.

- The **Paper Size** and **Source** settings should rarely need changing – if you've set your printer properties correctly. If you are printing on card or special paper, change the **Source** to *Manual*, if the option is available.

- In the **Orientation** area, *Portrait* is the normal way up; use *Landscape* if you want to print with the paper sideways.

- The **Margins** set the overall limits to the printable area. You can use the indents to reduce the width of text within the margins, but you cannot extend out beyond them.

- Click the **Printer** button to reach its **Properties** panel to change any settings at that level – you might, for example, want to switch to a lower resolution for printing a draft copy, or a higher resolution for the final output. (At low resolution, the printer will work faster and use less ink or toner.)

Figure 14.3 The **Page Setup** panel in WordPad.

This is Portrait Orientation.

Measurements here are in inches, but can be changed on the **Options** panel that opens from the **View** menu.

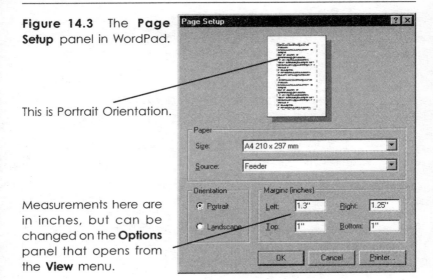

Graphics and other objects

WordPad is not limited to text only. Pictures, graphs, spreadsheets, audio and video clips – in fact just about any object that can be produced by any Windows application – can be incorporated into a WordPad document. The technique is much the same for any object.

1 Open the **Insert** menu and select **Object...**

2 If the object does not yet exist, select the **Object Type** and click **OK**.

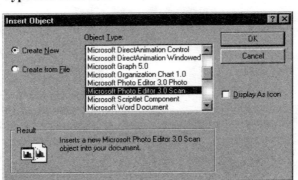

The appropriate application will open. When you have created the object, save it if you want to keep a separate copy for future use, then select the new **Exit & Return to Document** option from the **File** menu.

3 If you want to use an existing object, select **Create from File**, and browse through your folders to locate it.

4 Back in your WordPad document, you can resize the object if necessary.

Select the object – it will be outlined with handles at the corners and mid-edges.

Point to a handle to get the double-headed arrow then drag in or out as required. The position of the object across the page can be set by using the alignment buttons.

You can't do fancy layouts with WordPad. An image can sit by itself, separate from the text above and below, or can be embedded in a single line. That's it.

Figure 14.4 Adjusting the size of an image in WordPad. An inserted object can be edited by double-clicking on it – this opens the source application. Use **Exit & Return** when you have finished editing.

Print Preview

Like almost all applications, WordPad has a Print Preview facility. Working on screen, it is often difficult to tell how a document will look on paper – you may not be able to see the full width of the page and you certainly won't be able to see the full height. Use the Preview to get a better idea of the printed output, before you commit it to paper. Are your images or headings large enough to make the impact that you want? Do you get awkward breaks in the text at the ends of pages? If you are happy with the look of your document, you can print from here by clicking the **Print** button, otherwise, click **Close** to return to WordPad for that final tweaking.

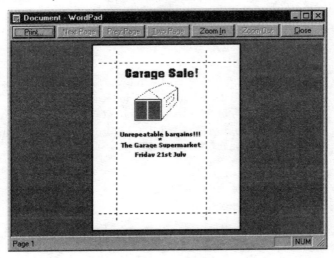

Figure 14.5 Using the Page preview facility to check the overall layout of a page. You can print from here, or close to return to editing.

Saving and opening files

In WordPad as in all applications you should save early and save often! Don't wait until you have finished writing that eight-page report before you save it. Applications can crash, hardware can fail, plugs get knocked out and we all make mistakes! The first save may take a few moments, but later saves are done at the click of a button.

To save a file for the first time:

    1 Open the **File** menu and select **Save As...**

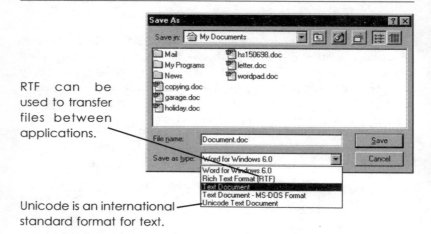

RTF can be used to transfer files between applications.

Unicode is an international standard format for text.

2 At the dialog box, select the folder.

3 Change the default 'Document' in the filename to something that will remind you what it is about.

4 If you want to save in a different format, pick one from the **Save as type** drop-down list.

5 Click **Save**.

To resave the current document:

1 Click – that's it!

When you close the document, or exit from WordPad, if you have not saved the document in its final state, you will be prompted to do so.

Next time that you want to work on the document, open it from the File menu. Either:

1 Select **Open** and then browse for the file – the dialog box is used in almost exactly the same way as the Save dialog box.

or If it is one of the files that you have used most recently, it will be listed at the bottom of the File menu. Just select it from here.

or If it is listed in the **Start → Documents** menu, open it from there.

14.3 Notepad

This is a text editor, not a word-processor. Text can be typed and edited here just as it can in WordPad, but it cannot be formatted. Because it is such a simple program, it starts up faster and uses less memory than any word-processor. It is the one to use if you want to produce plain text files – such as memos, program code and text which is to be handed on to someone else for formatting.

Figure 14.6 Editing a program in Notepad. You can set the font, but only for the screen display of all the text.

Apart from the normal File and Edit commands, the only significant facility offered by Notepad is a search routine – useful in programming for tracking down variables.

> **Search → Find...** opens the **Find** panel, where you can specify what to look for.

Search → Find Next simply repeats the last search.

14.4 Character Map

You will find **Character Map** on the **System Tools** menu – don't ask me why! It's a useful tool and one that I like to have close to hand. It allows you to see the characters available in any font, and to copy individual characters from there into a document.

1 Pick a font from the drop-down list – Symbol, webdings and Wingdings are the main fonts for decorative characters, and you will find foreign letters and mathematical symbols in most other fonts.

2 Hold down the left button and move across the display – the character under the cursor will be enlarged.

3 If you want to copy characters into a document, first click **Select** – the current one will be added to the **Characters to copy** display – then click **Copy** when you have all you want. Return to your document and use **Edit → Paste** – the character will be copied in, formatted to the chosen font.

or make a note of the **Keystroke** in the bottom right corner. If it says 'Alt+...', you can get that character by holding down **Alt** and typing the numbers (with the leading 0) into the *Number keypad*. Remember that the appearance of the character depends upon the font.

Hold down the button for an enlargement

Select first, then Copy

Figure 14.7 Character Map. If you are likely to want to use a character regularly, make a note of its **Keystroke**.

14.5 Paint

Graphics software falls into two broad groups. With some, including Paint, the image is produced by applying colour to a background – with each new line overwriting anything that may be beneath. Using these is very like real painting. You may be able to wipe out a mistake while the paint is still wet, but as soon as it has dried it is fixed on the canvas. (Paint allows you to undo the last move; some will let you backtrack further.)

The second type works with objects – lines, circles, text notes, etc. – that remain separate, and can be moved, deleted, recoloured and otherwise changed at any point. **Imaging** works this way (see page 201).

I use Paint regularly – it's the ideal tool for trimming and tidying screenshots for books! However, I don't expect that many of you will want it for this purpose. Though it can be used to produce intricate images, these require a great deal of time and skill – and can be created more successfully on a computer art package, with a full set of shading, shaping and manipulating tools. Paint is probably best used to draw simple diagrams, or as a children's toy, or to get an idea of how this type of graphics software works.

Figure 14.8 Using Paint to create a diagram. The **Text toolbar** gives you the full range of fonts and the main style effects.

The Toolbox

There is a simple but adequate set of tools. A little experimentation will
show how they all work.

Free-Form select | Select rectangle
Eraser | Fill with colour
Pick Colour | Magnifier
Pencil | Brush
Airbrush | Text
Line | Curve
Closed shapes { Rectangle | Polygon
Oval | Rounded rectangle

Transparent background
Opaque background   Option area

Most of them have options that can be set in the area below the toolbar.

- When you select an area (or paste an image from file or from
  the Clipboard) the background can be transparent or opaque.
- You can set the size of the Eraser, Brush, Airbrush, Line and
  Curve. N.B. The Line thickness applies to the closed shapes.
- The Magnifier is 4x by default, but can be 2x, 6x or 8x.
- The Pencil is only ever 1 pixel wide.
- Closed shapes can be outline or fill only, or both.

The Curve is probably the trickiest of the tools to use. The line can have
one or two curves to it.

1 Draw a line between the points
   where the curve will start and end.

2 Drag to create the first curve –
   pulling it up to about twice as far
   as you want the finished curve.

3 If the line is to have a second curve,
   drag it out now – as long as the
   mouse button is down, the line will
   flex to follow the cursor.

4 For a simple curve, just click at the
   end of the line.

UNDO IT!

If you go wrong any time – and you will with the Curve – use
Edit → Undo. This removes the effect of the last action.

Working with selected areas

The rectangular and free-form selectors can be used to select an area of
the screen. Once selected, an area can be:

- Deleted – use this for removing mistakes and excess bits.
- Copied – handy for creating repeating patterns.
- Saved as a file – use **Edit → Copy To...** and give a filename.
- Dragged elsewhere on screen.
- Flipped (mirrored) horizontally or vertically, or rotated in
  90° increments – use **Image → Flip/Rotate** for these effects.
- Stretched – to enlarge, shrink or distort, or skewed, either
  horizontally or vertically – use **Image → Stretch/Skew**.

Colours

The colour palette is used in almost the same way in all Windows programs.
You can select a colour from the basic set – use the left button for the
foreground colour and the right button for the background – or you can
mix your own colours.

Double-click on a colour in the **Color Box** or use **Colors → Edit Colors**
to open the **Edit Colors** panel. Initially only the **Basic colors** will be visible.
Click **Define Custom Colors** to open the full panel.

To define a new colour, drag the cross-hair cursor in the main square to set
the Red/Green/Blue balance, and move the arrow up or down the left scale
to set the light/dark level. Colours can also be set by typing in values, but
note that you are mixing light, not paint. Red and green make yellow; red,
green and blue make grey/white; the more you use, the lighter the colour.

When you have the colour you want, click **Add to Custom Colors**. The
new colour will replace the one currently selected in the Color Box on the
main screen.

Set the Red/
Green/Blue
balance.

Light/dark

Figure 14.9 Editing colours in Paint.

Filing

Saving and opening files is the same here as in WordPad. You can also use
Edit → Copy To... to save part of an image (see page 199) and **Edit →
Paste From...** to open a file so that you can combine its image with the
existing picture. The image will come in as a selected area, which can be
positioned wherever required. Set the background to transparent to merge
the two images, or to opaque for the new file to overlay the old image.

SCREENSHOTS

If you press the **Prt Sc** (Print Screen) key, the full screen display
will be copied into the Clipboard. Press **Alt** + **Prt Sc** and the
current window will be copied. The image can then be pasted
into Paint, or any other graphics program, and saved from
there. That's how the screenshots were produced for this book.

14.6 Imaging

You can use this to take images from a scanner or from file, and add simple annotations to them. And the annotations are simple. Text can be added on a transparent background, or on a yellow 'Post-It' note. There are drawing tools only for freehand or straight lines, and filled or open rectangles – so you are not going to be doing much more than simple diagrams with these!

When you use a tool, the object appears in the default colour, thickness and font. These can be changed by right-clicking on the object and selecting **Properties** form the shortcut menu. The defaults for a tool can be changed by right-clicking on its button and opening its **Properties** panel – well worth doing if you want to use the same tool several times with the same effects.

One of the interesting aspects of this program is the way that the image is formed. Each note, line or rectangle is a separate object. You can click on it at any point and move, resize or delete it, or change its colour, font or thickness. This is true even after the image has been saved and reopened.

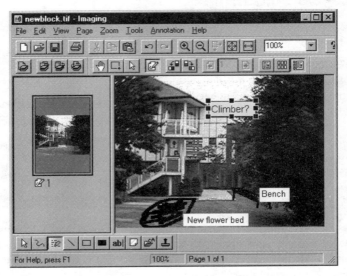

Figure 14.10 Using Imaging to annotate a scanned picture. The screen is seen here in **Page and Thumbnail View**. Switch to **Page View** and increase the **Zoom** level for close-up work.

Imaging has a few, limited editing facilities: you can cut, copy and paste rectangular areas, and the whole image can be rotated.

On the positive side, Imaging can read images in most major formats and can save as TIFF files (a high quality and very portable format, handled by many applications), as BMPs (like Paint) and AWD (fax format). You can use it to create multi-page documents, and these can be printed, faxed or e-mailed.

Figure 14.11 A typical **Properties** panel in Imaging. The **Palette** button opens the same **Edit Colors** panel that you met in Paint.

14.7 Calculator

Pack away that pocket calculator. You don't need it on your desk now that you have one on your Desktop!

The Calculator can work in two modes – Standard or Scientific. In either case, you use them the same way that you would a hand-held one. Enter the numbers, arithmetic operators and functions either by clicking on the screen keys, or by using your keyboard. (If you want to use the keyboard in the Scientific mode, look in the Help file for the keyboard equivalents.)

It has the same limitations as a pocket calculator – you can only store one value in memory at a time (**MS** to store it, **M+** to add to the value in memory, **MR** to recall it and **MC** to clear it); and you cannot print your results. If you want more than this, use a spreadsheet!

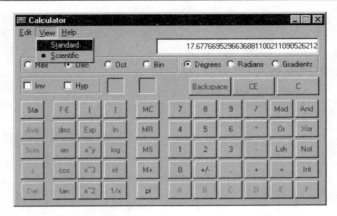

Figure 14.12 The Calculator in Scientific mode. In either mode, it works to 32 digit accuracy – is that close enough for you?

14.8 Phone Dialer

Phone Dialer is on the **Programs** → **Accessories** → **Communications** menu. To use it, you must have your modem plugged into the phone line. To use it conveniently, you should have a phone on your desk.

You can dial a number here, rather than on the phone, but that's scarcely worth doing unless the phone keypad is difficult to reach for some reason.

The real benefit of Phone Dialer is in the **Speed dial** facility, which can act as an extension to, or in place of, any memory buttons on the phone. (Setting up and changing Speed dial numbers here is far simpler than on my phone!) Up to 8 numbers can be stored.

To set up a Speed dial number:

1 Click on an unused Speed dial button.

2 Enter the **Name** and **Number**.

3 Click **Save**, or **Save and Dial** if you want to call immediately.

To edit a number:

1 Open the **Edit** menu and select **Speed Dial...**

2 Click on the button.

3 Edit and click **Save**.

■ New numbers can be set up here – click a blank button to start.

To make a Speed Dial call:

1 Click on the button.

2 When you get through, click **Talk** at the prompt.

3 When you have done, click **Hang up**.

The **Dialing** prompt appears as soon as the modem starts work. You can click **Hang Up** any time after you have connected – as long as you have the phone off the hook you will stay online.

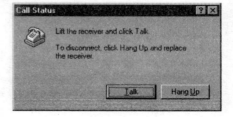

On the **Call Status** prompt, click **Talk** when you get through, or **Hang up** if there's no reply.

14.9 CD Player

Music while you work? Why not! Even cheap PC speakers produce a reasonable level and quality of sound.

To simply play a disc straight through could not be easier. Put the CD into the drive, Windows 98 will detect it, recognise that it is an audio disc and start the CD Player automatically.

- If you want to adjust the volume, click on the speaker icon in the far right of the Taskbar and pull the slider up or down as needed.
- If you need instant quiet at any point, click the Mute checkbox.

A lot more control is available, if wanted. Click on the CD Player button on the Taskbar to open its display.

If you want to set the order of play, or repeat or omit some tracks, open the **Disc** menu and select **Edit Play List...** (see Figure 14.13).

It's worth taking time over this, as any choices or other information that you enter here are recorded by Windows in a file (on the hard disk – it can't write to the CD) and will be reused next time the same CD is loaded.

- Select tracks from **Play List** and click **Remove->**, or from **Available Tracks** and click **<-Add**.
- To adjust the order, select a track and drag it up or down the list – an arrow to the left of the list indicates the position.
- If you like, you can replace the *Track...* identifier with a name. Select the from the **Available Tracks** list, type a name into the box at the bottom and click **Set Name**.
- Click **OK** when you have finished.

Figure 14.13 Editing the **Play List** in CD Player. If you also enter the **Artist** and **Title** here, they will be shown in the CD Player display.

Play options

On the Options menu you can select from:

- **Random Order** – if you want the excitement of not knowing what comes next!
- **Continuous Play** – loops back to the start after the last track.
- **Intro Play** – plays 10 seconds of each in turn.

14.10 Media Player

Media Player is a multi-purpose audio/video player. It can handle sound files in MIDI and in the native Windows format, WAVE – as well as audio CDs – or video in the standard Video for Windows (AVI) or the many ActiveMovie formats.

Newer, faster hardware and more efficient software has improved the quality of videos on PC, but not to the extent that I would want to spend much time looking at them.

It's essential for use with any multimedia package, and useful for viewing the demos and samples that you will find on the Windows 98 CD – and on the CDs that grace the covers of PC magazines. There are also lots of video clips available on the Internet, but I'm not sure how many are worth the download time. 1Mb of video gives you around 7 seconds of playing time, and will take up to 10 minutes to download – and you must have the whole file on your disk before you can start to play it. (With the new 'streaming video' technology, now coming into use on the Web, the videos are played as they are downloaded. The images are jerkier, but at least you don't have to wait to see whether they are worth watching at all.)

Sorry, I've been rather negative about this. Let's close on a positive note. One very neat feature of Media Player is that it allows you to mark off a section which can then be copied into a document, and played from there.

1 Go to the start of the section and click ▾.

2 Move to the end and click ▴.

3 Open the **Edit** menu and select **Copy Object**.

4 Switch to your document application (e.g. Word) and use **Edit ➜ Paste** or **Paste Special**.

5 Anyone reading the document can then play the selected clip by double clicking on the video object.

Section marked for copying

Figure 14.14 Viewing a video clip in Media Player.

14.11 My Briefcase

If you use the same documents in two machines – whether they are a desktop and laptop PC or PC at home and work – My Briefcase can simplify the business of keeping copies up to date.

Here's how it is used when working on two separate PCs, with the briefcase transferred via a floppy disk. The process is similar – and slightly simpler – when you have a PC lap-linked to a mobile computer.

1 Use My Computer or Explorer to locate each document that you want to work on elsewhere.

2 Right-click on the document and select **Send To → My Briefcase**. It will be copied into the briefcase folder.

3 When you have all your documents together, right-click on the My Briefcase folder on the Desktop and select **Send To → Floppy (A:)**. The folder is moved onto the disk.

4 At the second machine, drag the My Briefcase folder from the floppy onto the Desktop. Leave the files in that folder and work on them there.

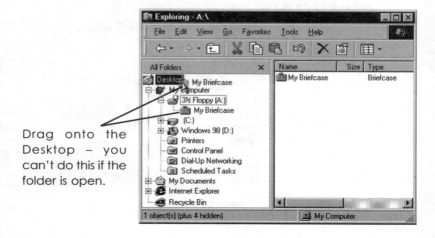

Drag onto the Desktop – you can't do this if the folder is open.

5 Drag the folder back onto the floppy before leaving the second machine.

6 Back at base, drag the My Briefcase folder onto the Desktop.

7 Open **My Briefcase** and check the status of the files. Any that have been edited will be marked **Needs updating** – select them, unless all need updating.

8 Open the **Briefcase** menu and select **Update All...** or **Update Selection**.

This was a new file saved in the Briefcase at the second machine.

9 At the **Update My Briefcase** panel, those files that have been changed will be marked for replacement. If you do not want to replace the original files, right click and select **Skip** or **Replace** (the Briefcase copy with the original). Click **Update**.

Update from the Briefcase copy

Restore the original

Don't update

14.12 Summary

- The techniques and skills that you learn using the accessories can be applied to many other Windows applications.
- WordPad has enough formatting and layout facilities to cope with many word-processing jobs.
- If you want only plain text output, Notepad will handle this very efficiently.
- Character Map will let you examine the characters in any font. Characters can be copied from here and pasted into documents.
- Paint is a simple graphics program that can be used for creating diagrams, fun pictures and for editing and saving screenshots.
- With Imaging you can add annotations to scanned or imported images.
- Calculator will do the job of a simple or a scientific pocket calculator.
- Use Phone Dialer to extend or replace the memory functions of your telephone.
- The CD Player plays CDs automatically, but also lets you select tracks and set the play order.
- Media Player can play audio CDs, computer sound files and videos.
- My Briefcase makes it easier to manage files if you need to work on them on two machines.

INDEX